2004
CHILDREN'S MISSION YEARBOOK
for prayer & study

A new commandment I give to you, that you love one another

The *Children's Mission Yearbook for Prayer & Study* is published by Witherspoon Press and the Mission Education and Promotion program team of Congregational Ministries Publishing, Congregational Ministries Division, a ministry of the General Assembly Council of the Presbyterian Church (U.S.A.). Jon Brown is senior editor/coordinator of Mission Education and Promotion. Sandra Moak Sorem is the publisher of Congregational Ministries Publishing.

A lot of people worked together to create this book! Christina Berry was the writer, Deborah Haines the editor, Billie Healy the associate editor, Nancy Goodhue the copy editor, Erin McGee the children's curriculum liaison, and Jeanne Williams the designer/art director. Margaret Hall Boone, Carol E. Johnson, Lily Osuamkpe, Susan Salsburg, and Mark Thomson also contributed greatly to the project.

The cover for this book was designed by Carol Cornette of Louisville, Kentucky. Her inspiration came from the cover of the *2004 Mission Yearbook for Prayer & Study*. Carol also did the illustrations throughout the book.

Where possible, the names of the people who took the photographs throughout the book can be found on the pages where the photos appear.

The Scripture verses that appear each week (except for the Special Offerings and General Assembly weeks) are part of the daily lectionary, taken from the *Book of Common Prayer*, with revisions that were made for inclusion in the *Lutheran Book of Worship*. Scripture quotations are from the New Revised Standard Version of the Bible, copyrighted 1989 by the Division of Christian Education of the National Council of the Churches of Christ in the U.S.A., and are used by permission.

Let us know what you think about the *2004 Children's Mission Yearbook for Prayer & Study!* Send us a letter to: *Children's Mission Yearbook for Prayer & Study*, Mission Education and Promotion, Presbyterian Church (U.S.A.), 100 Witherspoon Street, Louisville, KY 40202-1396. Or send us an e-mail to: dhaines@ctr.pcusa.org. Call us toll free at (888) 728-7228, ext. 5170.

You can order more copies of this book for your friends! Ask your teacher or parent to call (800) 524-2612 and ask for PDS #70-612-04-451. The cost is $5.50 each or $4.00 each for 10 or more.

A Message from the Moderator

photo by Danny Bolin

Dear girls and boys:

Many of you were baptized when you were little babies. Your pastor splashed water on your head and then blessed you in the name of Jesus. The water was a symbol of grace—the free, energetic gift of God's love to you. We believe that each of you is special, precious, and cherished forever. And so are all God's children.

Just before Jesus said goodbye to his first disciples, he gave them a new commandment, a new way he wanted all of them—and us—to act in our lives. He told them "to love one another." And then he showed them what this kind of love looks like. He got down on his knees and washed the feet of each disciple. The disciples were very surprised at his action. Why? Because in those days all the roads were dusty and everyone wore sandals. And only servants washed the dirty feet of guests. What an amazing thing for Jesus to do—to serve the ordinary needs of ordinary people! As those who follow Jesus, we are called to do the same.

The *Children's Mission Yearbook* gives us pictures of modern-day disciples who are loving God's people around the world. You will be challenged as you read stories about feeding the hungry, helping children, building schools, and teaching the Bible, often in far away places. But everything you will read or see are stories about love—about loving God's people the way God loves each of us. Have fun!

Blessings to you in the name of our Lord, our Savior, and our Friend, Jesus Christ!

—Rev. Susan R. Andrews, moderator, 215th General Assembly, Presbyterian Church (U.S.A.)

Suggestions for Using This Book

How you use your *Children's Mission Yearbook* depends on you. Every two pages cover one week in 2004. You might choose to do all of the activities for a week at one time. You might choose one activity to do each day until you have done them all in a week's time. You might choose to do the same activity each day. For example, we encourage you to pray each week's prayer every day. Some activities will take longer than a week to do. You will need an adult to help you with some activities, especially when you want to try one of the recipes! However you decide to use the book, we hope you will make it your own book and learn as much as you can about being a Presbyterian and how Presbyterians are involved with mission all around the world. And, we hope that you have fun as you learn!

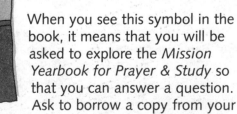

When you see this symbol in the book, it means that you will be asked to explore the *Mission Yearbook for Prayer & Study* so that you can answer a question. Ask to borrow a copy from your pastor, teacher, or parent. Better yet, ask them to help you find the answers to the questions!

Scripture

The verse each week is from the Daily Lectionary. Do you know what lectionary means? It's a list of Bible readings for every day. If you look in a *Mission Yearbook for Prayer & Study* you will see that each day has a Daily Lectionary. There is also a Sunday Lectionary. Can you find one?

MISSION IN THE UNITED STATES

Presbytery name

Each week there's a story about a different presbytery. It will always be a presbytery in the synod listed at the bottom of the page. A list of all the synods and presbyteries in the PC(USA) can be found on the inside back cover.

Craft or Recipe or Word Puzzle

You will discover one new activity every week. Sometimes it's a craft, sometimes a recipe, and sometimes a word puzzle. Be sure to ask an adult to help you with the recipes that mention you'll need adult help. Have fun with these!

Word of the Week

The Word of the Week is a special word chosen just for that week! You may already know what it means but you will learn more. Look for it in the stories or elsewhere on its page!

Each week a face or animal can be found on the two pages. Can you spot them?

What You Can Do

You can find some ideas for things you can do for others that are related to the stories you have read on each week's two pages. You might think of other ideas.

PRAYER

We hope you will pray for the people you read about each week. We have given a prayer for you to use every day—or you can use your own.

MISSION AROUND THE WORLD

Country name

What kinds of mission work are Presbyterians doing in countries besides the United States? You can find out here. The country featured will always be in the world area listed at the bottom of the right page.

Did You Know?

You can learn something new about one of the stories on the page when you read this section.

Giving What You Have

One of the important things about being a Presbyterian is giving regularly to the church. This is one of the ways we give back to God and support work around the world done in God's name by Presbyterians. We can be generous with our ideas, our time, and our support. In this section we give you some suggestions for giving to your church.

We are members of the Presbyterian Church (U.S.A.). The abbreviation for that is PC(USA), which is what we use in the book. Another abbreviation we use is Rev., which means Reverend. That's the title we use for ministers, as in the Rev. Jill Church.

MISSION IN THE UNITED STATES

Carlisle Presbytery

Pennsylvania

Kids who live near Capital Presbyterian Church in Harrisburg, Pennsylvania, have Kids' Haven to go to after school. In May 2002, the Rev. SanDawna Ashley, a pastor with a dream, shared the idea for Kids' Haven with Capital Presbyterian Church, a 144-year-old African American congregation with ninety-six members. She told them that neighborhood youth needed a safe and fun place to go after school. At Kids' Haven they do have fun! Monday through Friday professional instructors teach classes in drama, art, martial arts, and African dance. Kids also take special Rites of Passage classes, where they learn the seven principles of Kwanzaa: unity, self-determination,

SCRIPTURE

Praise the LORD! I will give thanks to the LORD with my whole heart (Psalm 111:1).

collective work and responsibility, cooperative economics, purpose, creativity, and faith. Many Kids' Haven students and their parents now attend worship at Capital Presbyterian Church. Kids' Haven is a gift to city youth in Harrisburg.

Find Carlisle Presbytery on the map on page 112.

Liturgical dancers from Kids' Haven share in worship at Capital Presbyterian Church.

Word Puzzle

We celebrate the birth of Christ through Epiphany, January 6. Unscramble each of the clue words that have to do with Christmas. Copy the letters in the numbered squares to other squares with the same number. Solve the puzzle and see what the psalm tells us to do!

GAMI

MASTSIRCH YJO RINGOFFE

DREPHSHES

RATS FO HEMLETHEB

GELANS

HENYAPIP

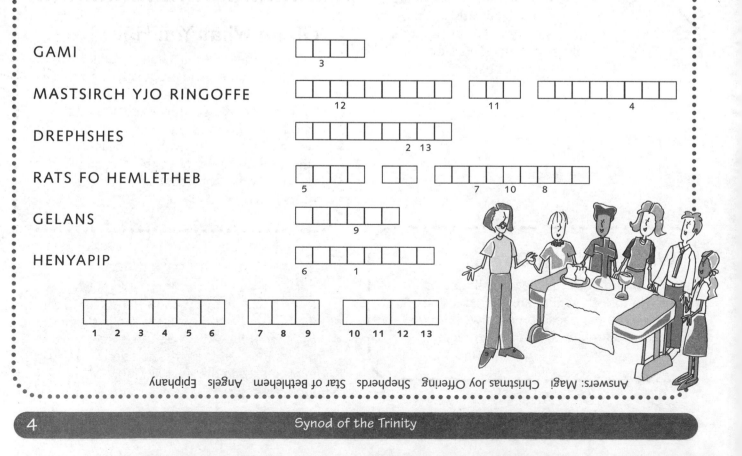

Answers: Magi: Christmas Joy Offering Shepherds Star of Bethlehem Angels Epiphany

MISSION AROUND THE WORLD

Bosnia and Herzegovina

Since 1997, Brett McMichael has been working on behalf of AGAPE, a group that helps children in Croatia and Bosnia and Herzegovina.

Brett works as a play therapist, using puppet and marionette theaters, drawing, painting, storytelling, and general play. Play therapy helps kids work out their fears and problems. Brett tells us about a visit he made to a special children's hospital: "Although there is a playroom in the hospital, I visited most of the children in their beds, as many are too sick and weak to come to the room. The social worker told me to pay a special visit to a boy who was eight years old. He used to be full of laughter, but lately he would just lie in his bed, almost motionless. I knew almost all boys of that age love helicopters so I brought him one and a couple of cars and trucks. Before I knew what was happening, he was busy spinning the propellers and making helicopter type sounds—the action was thrilling and exciting as we rescued vehicles stranded under heavy boulders and collapsed ice caves (well, actually pillows and layers of sheets and blankets!). As I saw him and other children happily playing with these toys, I felt proud to be a part of such a wonderful project. God blessed me so much that day!"

Find Bosnia and Herzegovina on the map on page 110.

Did You Know?

Bosnia and Herzegovina used to be part of a country called Yugoslavia. In the 1990s some of the states that formed Yugoslavia decided they wanted to be separate countries. A civil war brought much destruction and harm to many people. Peace came in 1995, but a lot of people still suffer from the effects of the war. AGAPE is a relief organization that is helping people in Bosnia and Herzegovina get back on their feet.

PRAYER

Loving God, as we begin a New Year, we thank you for the gift of faith. Help us to believe even when we cannot see, and to live our faith in mission for you. In Jesus' name. Amen.

Did You Know?

The moderator of the 215th General Assembly (2003) of the PC(USA) is the Rev. Susan R. Andrews. Did you read her special message to you on page 3? You can find another message from Ms. Andrews in the *2004 Mission Yearbook for Prayer & Study*.

Word of the Week — Faith

Faith is believing, even when we do not see. It is acting as if something is so even though we can't prove it.

What You Can Do

The Presbyterians at Capital Presbyterian Church live their faith by making a great place where kids can do creative things after school. Brett McMichael lives his faith by playing and doing creative things with children. Take time each day this week to pray for kids everywhere, and live your faith wherever you are.

Giving What You Have

Make a plan now to give to missions through your church every month this year. You can make a pledge to your church (that's a promise of the amount you will give) or you can use the suggestions in this book.

MISSION IN THE UNITED STATES
Presbytery of Beaver Butler
Pennsylvania

Have you ever been to church camp? How far away did you go? Can you imagine going as far away as Nepal for church camp? Sangam "Sam" Napit came to Westminster Highlands church camp in the Presbytery of Beaver Butler all the way from Nepal.

(Can you find the Presbytery of Beaver Butler on the map on page 112 and Nepal on the map on page 110?) He came to be a camp counselor but he was a teacher, too. "I was baptized when I was fourteen and that is when I gave my life to the Lord," Sam said. At camp, Sam showed the campers how to write their names in Nepalese. He cooked a meal that consisted of chicken curry, pilau (a rice dish), and yogurt with bananas for dessert. The campers ate with their hands as do most Nepalese villagers. Sam wrote, "I was able to talk about Nepal and share about the culture. We also compared Hinduism and Christianity, and talked about the differences in the faiths. I am sure my campers' faith grew stronger when they were able to hear from someone who had experienced a different culture but the same faith."

What You Can Do

Learn about camps and conferences in your presbytery, then share the information with others in your church by giving a minute for mission during a service or church meeting. (When you do, remember to add some leaves to your tree.)

SCRIPTURE

Clap your hands, all you peoples; shout to God with loud songs of joy (Psalm 47:1).

Craft
Sharing Tree

Have you ever read the book by Shel Silverstein called *The Giving Tree*? The more the tree shared the smaller it became until it was only a stump. But a sharing tree grows the more you share. A sharing tree is a tree you can add to as you share in mission. Make a sharing tree to use all during 2004.

Materials

brown paper (Old paper grocery
    sacks will work fine.)
green paper
tape or glue
pencil
markers or crayons
stickers (optional)

First, cut out a tree trunk and branches from the brown paper. If you are making a very big tree, you may have to cut out pieces of your trunk and branches and then glue or tape them together. Find a place to put the tree where you will see it often. The back of a door is often a good place. Make sure it is okay to put your tree there for a whole year. Use the green paper to cut out leaves. Each week, add a leaf or two to the tree for something you have shared with someone. Write or draw something on the leaf to remind you of your sharing. At the end of the year your tree will be green and leafy and covered with SHARING!

MISSION AROUND THE WORLD

Serbia and Montenegro

Find a map of Europe and see if you can find the small country of Serbia and Montenegro. István Csete-Szemesi is bishop of the Reformed Church in Serbia and Montenegro. There was war and trouble in Serbia and Montenegro for ten years. Even though the war ended in October 2000 and many changes have been made in the government, there are still problems. Many of the older people who are church members of the Reformed Church do not have enough money to buy food and clothes. Some have no income at all. The elders of the church bring help. They ask the members who have more to share with those who have less. In winter they bring food and supplies in a horse-drawn sleigh, sharing God's love by sharing food and clothing.

Church elders deliver food, clothing, and household items by sleigh to those who are housebound.

PRAYER

Loving God, help us to share your love with others through prayer, giving, and our work in missions. Bless those in Serbia and Montenegro who bring your love in a horse-drawn sleigh, and bless all the Presbyterian camps where children learn more about you. In Jesus' name. Amen.

Giving What You Have

For each of the special persons who visited the Christ child on Epiphany put 30 cents into the offering plate on Sunday.

El Día De Los Tres Reyes

Word of the Week
Epiphany

On January 6, Christians celebrate Epiphany. In Latin American countries, it is called *El Día De Los Tres Reyes.* That is Spanish for "Three Kings Day." With that as your clue, can you remember what we celebrate on Epiphany?

MISSION IN THE UNITED STATES
Lehigh Presbytery
Pennsylvania

What do two neighbors do when a need exists right along their borders? They do what the Lehigh and Lackawanna Presbyteries have done. They share their resources and make a new church—right between them! They also share a vision. Both presbyteries give money and support to New Life Presbyterian Church, a new church in Mt. Pocono, Pennsylvania. Find these two presbyteries on the map on page 112.

The Rev. Jeffrey Cochran-Carney and the Rev. Cynthia Cochran-Carney were called as founding pastors. They like music, and they like using music to reach out to others. They held a Mardi Gras Jazz Sunday, and eight new families came to worship! It was a great Sunday morning worship service with Dixieland jazz music, Mardi Gras decorations, helium balloons, and lots of food. Even though it snowed and rained the night before, sixty-five people came. The children helped celebrate by wearing masks and marching through the church while the band played "When the Saints Go Marching In." God's Spirit is creating new life in a new place!

Did You Know?
Mardi Gras is on February 24 this year. Mardi Gras (French for "Fat Tuesday") is the day before Ash Wednesday, which is the first day of Lent.

SCRIPTURE

Create in me a clean heart, O God, and put a new and right spirit within me (Psalm 51:10).

Recipe
Harissa

Harissa is a spicy hot condiment or seasoning from the Middle East.

Ingredients

1/2 tsp. caraway seeds
1 tbs. cayenne pepper
1/2 tbs. ground cumin
1/2 tsp. salt
1 small clove garlic, finely minced
2 tbs. fat-free Italian salad dressing

Grind caraway seeds in coffee grinder or mini-food processor, or by using a mortar and pestle. Mix caraway seeds, cayenne pepper, cumin, and salt together. Add garlic and mix. Add dressing and mix well. Store covered in the refrigerator. A little goes a long way.

Italian Dressing

Cayenne Pepper

What You Can Do

Pray each day this week for the people of Tunisia. Give thanks to God for all of God's work in the world. And be sure to look for creative ways to share God's love.

Children from New Life Presbyterian Church celebrate Mardi Gras Jazz Sunday by wearing masks and marching through the congregation while the band plays "When the Saints Go Marching In."

Lehigh Presbytery has a Presbyterian-related college within its bounds. Find the name of the college by looking in the Mission Yearbook for Prayer & Study on the page about Lehigh Presbytery (page 12). Are there any Presbyterian-related colleges near where you live? Look in Appendix A of the Mission Yearbook and see if any are in cities near you.

Word of the Week

Create

God creates new things, and so can we. With God's love we create new ways of living and sharing.

PRAYER

Do you play a musical instrument? If you do, think of a piece of music you love and play it for God as a kind of prayer. Or sing a song you love in the same way, as an offering to God.

MISSION AROUND THE WORLD

Tunisia

Some countries around the world have laws that don't let Christian groups talk about their faith. Those groups have to be creative. Since they aren't allowed to talk about God's love, they have to think of ways to show God's love. A group called the Association for Cooperation in Tunisia (ACT) has been working for more than twenty years to act in ways that show God's love in Tunisia. They give small loans to rural women so they can start their own small businesses. They help people give care to babies whose parents have abandoned them. They help care for people who are physically disabled and for children with learning difficulties. The people who work to show God's love in Tunisia ask us, "Please join us in praying that we will continue to bring about the kingdom of God in this place through reaching out and showing love in practical ways to those who most need to know Christ's love." Find Tunisia on the map on page 110.

Giving What You Have

Pay attention this week to the many ways that you see love shown without words. Put 5 cents into your church offering plate on Sunday for each creative expression of love that you see.

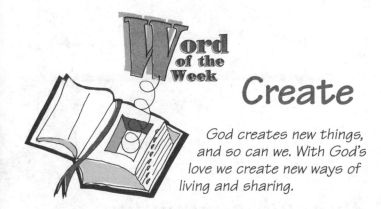

MISSION IN THE UNITED STATES

Presbytery of Eastern Oklahoma

In the summer of 2002, the youth from John Calvin Presbyterian Church and John Knox Presbyterian Church took a trip to Heifer Ranch. They traveled from Tulsa, Oklahoma, to the headquarters of Heifer Project International in Perryville, Arkansas. (Look on the map on page 112 to find Arkansas and the Presbytery of Eastern Oklahoma.) They took the trip so they could do mission work and become aware of how some people around the world have to make do with so little. The youth came back to Tulsa ready to help in any way they could. They decided to have a Quarter Project. Adults of the church helped them build tubes that would hold "towers" of quarters. When a tower was full, there were enough quarters in it to buy one sheep. The kids also made towers for a trio of rabbits, a flock of chickens, and a heifer. Every week the tubes were in the church so that passers-by could donate their extra quarters. After only six months, the youth had enough quarters to buy all four kinds of animals: the sheep, the rabbits, the chickens, and the heifer! The project raised more than $800, almost all in quarters! The entire church was able to participate in an activity that would benefit people around the world.

What You Can Do

Heifer Project International has a program for kids to read books and raise money to help others get farm animals so they can have the food they need. You can learn all about it at www.readtofeed.org.

Word of the Week

Spirit

Spirit is "energy in action." God's Spirit in us means we put our energy into action to do God's work.

SCRIPTURE

"God is spirit, and those who worship [God] must worship in spirit and truth" (John 4:24).

Craft

Helping Heavenly Host

Use this angel pattern, or one you make yourself, to cut out angels from lightweight cardboard. Make wings for your angels. You can make wings of tissue paper, coffee filters, or paper doilies. Decorate the wings using watercolor markers, then spray them with a fine mist of water for a tie-dye look. After the wings are dry, glue or tape them to the angel. Use a piece of yarn or ribbon to hang the angels up. Maybe you and your church school class can make some and ask people at church to donate money to a mission project for each angel they take home!

Did You Know?

The Heifer Project, like the International Center of Bethlehem, works because it helps people to help themselves. It has helped 4 million families in 115 countries move closer to independence by giving them one of 25 types of breeding livestock to use for plowing or for food and income (from milk or eggs).

PRAYER

Spirit God, you are always with us. Let us remember what your angels sang: Peace on earth. Give us the energy to serve you and to help others know your peace. In Jesus' name. Amen.

Read More About It

You can read about Heifer Project International on the Web at www.heifer.org or in the book *Beatrice's Goat*.

Poem

Spirit

Spirit of God I feel you here
    sometimes when I
Pray or when I sing
I know that you are here and
    everywhere
Rising in our songs and in our
    prayers
I know that I am part of you and
    you are part of God, the
Trinity: Creator, Redeemer,
    Sustainer.

MISSION AROUND THE WORLD
Israel/Palestine/Jerusalem

In the last three years Bethlehem, the town where Jesus was born, has seen much violence and destruction. Israeli army tanks have been roaming the streets of this little town where angels once sang "peace on earth." Many buildings have been destroyed. Many people now have no jobs. The International Center of Bethlehem, an outreach ministry of the Evangelical Lutheran Christian Church and a partner of the PC(USA), has started a new ministry. They train Palestinian women who have no jobs to create angels made of pieces of glass from buildings that have been destroyed. The women carefully pick up pieces of glass from among the rubble and then use the glass to make angels at the International Center's art workshops. These glass angels are purchased by many congregations throughout the world and continue to provide a source of income for many women who do not have jobs in Bethlehem today.

Bethlehem is in Israel. Can you find Israel on the map on page 110?

Palestinian women make angels from the rubble of war.

Giving What You Have

For each egg in your refrigerator, offer 10 minutes of your time to help a neighbor, someone in your congregation, or around your home.

MISSION IN THE UNITED STATES

Presbytery of South Louisiana

The Presbytery of South Louisiana is located just north of the Gulf of Mexico, which means it is often in the path of hurricanes and tropical storms. Find it on the map on page 112. In a local newspaper column a journalist wrote, "The good thing about Louisiana is that we only have hurricanes once a week." Hurricanes hardly happen that often; but when they do occur, the churches in Louisiana are ready to help with the clean-up and healing. Recently two powerful storms hit back to back. Tropical Storm Isidore came on September 26, 2002, and Hurricane Lili arrived just one week later. The two storms did damage to more than seventy thousand structures. News reports said that over eighty thousand

SCRIPTURE

[God] heals the brokenhearted, and binds up their wounds (Psalm 147:3).

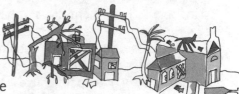

people suffered damage due to the storms. People will be cleaning up after these storms for years. Many people in the region live simply. One man lived on his shrimp boat until Hurricane Lili sank it near the banks of the bayou. He now lives in a one-room hut, about six feet by six feet; but with the support of his family and friends, he will stay in the area because it is home. When disaster strikes, healing can come in many forms. Churches of the presbytery have helped with clean-up and coordinating relief efforts. First Presbyterian Church of Thibodaux, Louisiana, built showers so that the church can host volunteers who come to help.

Word Puzzle: Y Words

Besides the E, the only vowel in Egypt is Y. Find the Y words in this puzzle. Shade in the squares of the words listed below. Words go across (and backward) and up and down, but not diagonally. We've shaded in YAV (the only word in the list with another vowel!) to get you started.

Y	M	G	Y	P	M	F	G	X	S	N	V	M	Y	R	R	H
Y	Y	P	S	Y	W	C	I	B	A	L	N	O	W	R	Y	Y
S	B	M	Y	G	A	R	I	P	B	X	Z	Y	H	W	H	O
Q	Q	G	F	R	Y	C	V	S	U	N	Y	L	F	Y	G	L
A	Y	E	Y	C	R	Y	A	Q	N	Y	H	T	C	G	D	M
V	H	A	T	P	T	H	P	M	Y	N	S	P	S	V	S	A
C	D	Z	G	Q	R	H	Y	T	H	M	S	L	N	A	C	X
B	E	V	M	A	D	Y	C	B	Y	Q	V	M	Z	E	V	C
U	H	J	L	W	K	H	R	L	X	A	T	O	U	R	X	E
I	M	I	K	D	J	J	Y	Y	N	Z	F	K	G	T	Z	F
M	L	L	J	B	B	S	P	M	Y	W	C	J	T	V	I	V
S	O	K	H	H	I	C	T	P	L	S	R	N	Y	K	X	B
K	S	F	A	U	K	O	M	H	H	Y	D	U	J	H	L	H
O	A	Q	S	M	M	L	Y	P	Y	E	X	H	N	M	L	N
P	Y	N	C	Z	P	N	T	R	M	F	I	B	X	Q	J	M
D	M	M	D	O	Q	M	H	Y	N	V	S	Q	L	A	N	R
F	O	P	O	L	Y	Y	Y	A	V	B	Z	G	Q	Z	M	T

Word list: BY CRY CRYPT FLY FRY GYM HYMN LYMPH LYNX MYRRH MYTH NYMPH PRY PYGMY RHYTHMS SHY SPY THY TRY WHY WRY YAV

MISSION AROUND THE WORLD

Egypt

Have you ever heard of a PC(USA) YAV? It sounds funny, unless you know that it stands for Presbyterian Church (U.S.A.) Young Adult Volunteer—YAV! Young Adult Volunteers are Presbyterians who are between the ages of nineteen and thirty and who give a year of their lives to serve people in communities around the world. In the fall of 2002, three young women came to the Synod of the Nile in Egypt. (Find Egypt on your map on page 110.)

The three young women—Cathy, Sherri, and Julie—were the first YAVs to be placed in Egypt. They called themselves "the daughters of the Nile." They taught math and music and helped in programs for refugees. The people of Egypt were glad to have young American Christians spend a year serving in the Synod of the Nile schools and health programs. They showed compassion for the most disadvantaged people of this society. Egyptians, both Christian and Muslim, were amazed that these young people would come as Christian volunteers in a country that many Americans perceive as dangerous. The work of these YAVs was truly a ministry of love and learning that continued when the young people returned to the United States after their year in Egypt.

The "daughters of the Nile"—Cathy, Sherri, and Julie—ride down the Nile with a boatman's help.

PRAYER

God, help us to be the ones who spread your healing love to everyone. Thank you for the work of YAVs in Egypt and around the world, and thank you for the healing work of the Presbytery of South Louisiana. In Jesus' name. Amen.

What You Can Do

The PC(USA) Young Adult Volunteers Web site at www.pcusa.org/missionconnections/yav has letters from YAVs around the world. If it is okay with your parents, send an e-mail to one of them!

Did You Know?

In 2003 about sixty young adults were serving in the United States and abroad through the Young Adult Volunteer (YAV) program. They serve through the National Ministries Division in Tucson, Arizona; West Yellowstone, Montana; Ketchikan, Alaska; Miami, Florida; Seattle, Washington; Cincinnati, Ohio; and Hollywood, California. They serve through the Worldwide Ministries Division in Guatemala, Kenya, Northern Ireland, Argentina, Ghana, Thailand, Egypt, Hungary, India, the Philippines, and the United Kingdom.

Giving What You Have

Count the many ways of healing you have read about on these two pages. For each one, give 10 cents to your church on Sunday.

Word of the Week **Healing**

Healing can be more than physical. Think of the many ways God's love can heal the hurts of the world!

MISSION IN THE UNITED STATES

Presbytery of Arkansas

Churches in the Presbytery of Arkansas are running the race with perseverance in several ways! First Presbyterian Church of Little Rock feeds homeless people in a soup kitchen. Other congregations in the city also volunteer to serve them hundreds of hot meals every week. First Presbyterian Church in Mena hosted college students during the Christmas holidays. Church members took them to the top of nearby Rich Mountain and showed them a beautiful part of God's world. The presbytery camp, Ferncliff, welcomed the children of imprisoned mothers to a program called Family Matters so they might feel supported and loved. The youth of the Presbytery of Arkansas helped raise money so that a Zambian student could continue her education at Lyon College in Batesville, Arkansas. She came to the United States to attend a camp for children who had experienced violence in their lives.

The Presbytery of Arkansas is partnering with two presbyteries in southern Mexico. It is working with one of the Mexican presbyteries to build a camp for youth. The partnership with the other presbytery is just beginning. The Presbytery of Arkansas also called a Hispanic pastor to work with new immigrants from Mexico who are streaming into the northwest corner of Arkansas. There they are encouraged through Bible study and pastoral care to remember the Lord their God in a strange new

SCRIPTURE

Therefore, since we are surrounded by so great a cloud of witnesses, . . . let us run with perseverance the race that is set before us (Hebrews 12:1).

What You Can Do

Memorize the Scripture verse for this week. When you feel like giving up, remember the verse and keep on trying.

Youth fill bags of bean soup mix to sell to raise money for a Zambian student's scholarship.

Giving What You Have

How many times this week will you run or race? Maybe you raced to the school bus, or maybe you had a race in spelling class. Count all the races and put 10 cents into the church offering plate for each race you run this week.

MISSION AROUND THE WORLD

Poland

Pop quiz! If there are 38 million people in Poland and 95 percent of them (or 36,100,000 people) are Roman Catholic, how many people are not Roman Catholic? (Answer: 1,900,000) The Evangelical Reformed Church is one of our PC(USA) partners in Poland. The Evangelical Reformed Church of Poland has approximately 4,500 members. It has 10 widely scattered parishes and seven preaching stations. One struggle for the church is that the congregations are spread out across wide distances. The pastor of the small parish in Zychlin, about 70 miles west of Warsaw, must travel roughly 750 miles to preach to all his assigned congregations. Meeting the worship needs of such small numbers of people across such distances requires perseverance.

The country of Poland is bordered on the north by the Baltic Sea and on the east by the republics of Lithuania, Belarus, and Ukraine. Can you find Poland on the map on page 110?

Did You Know?

In the United States, the word *parish* refers to a congregation. In a country like Poland, a parish is a geographical area. Poland, which is slightly smaller than the state of New Mexico, has only 10 parishes.

PRAYER

God, bless the churches of Poland and of the Presbytery of Arkansas. Help them, and me, to persevere and never give up on helping others. In Jesus' name. Amen.

Recipe

Pierogi

Ingredients

2 cups all-purpose flour
1/2 tsp. salt
1 tsp. vegetable oil
pinch (1/8 tsp.) baking powder
1 egg, beaten
1/2 cup warm water

A favorite traditional food from Poland is pierogis. To make the dough, mix together the flour, salt, and baking powder in a large bowl. In another bowl mix together the vegetable oil and beaten egg. Pour into the dry ingredients and mix. Knead dough for 8 to 10 minutes. Cover the bowl with a towel and let the dough rest for about an hour. Roll out with a rolling pin. Then cut into circles about 4 inches in diameter. Place a teaspoon of filling in the center of each circle. You can fill the dumplings with mashed potatoes, meat, cheese, or fruit pie filling. Wet your fingertips, fold the circle over, and use the water to seal the edges. Cook for a few minutes in gently boiling water. Some people like to fry the fruit dumplings for a minute or two on each side then sprinkle powdered sugar on them.

Word of the Week

Perseverance

Perseverance means to keep on trying, or to stick with a job until it is done. God wants us to have perseverance in prayer and in helping to share the good news.

MISSION IN THE UNITED STATES

Presbytery of Sierra Blanca

New Mexico

Imagine a simple little house in the middle of a low-income neighborhood of Sunland Park, New Mexico. This little house used to be a terrible place, filled with drug abuse and violence. All that changed when Cristo Rey Outreach helped community residents turn the house into a neighborhood center, a sign of hope. Now at La Casita (Spanish for "the little house") you will find a Girl Scout troop, after-school tutoring, a Christian education program, and quiet space for children to read, make art projects, and work on one of the donated computers. Grown-ups can participate in a food-buying cooperative, classes to learn how to be a U.S. citizen, a Spanish-language camp, and programs for area pastors. Rosa Nuñez lives in the community and works to organize local women in everything from economic development to Bible study. Every spring and summer Cristo Rey hosts mission work groups. The work groups do construction and lead youth activities while they learn first-hand about the border region of the United States and Mexico. Find the Presbytery of Sierra Blanca on the map on page 112.

La Casita

Word of the Week

Marvelous

Marvelous means "causing wonder or astonishment; miraculous; wonderful; of the highest or best kind or quality; first-rate." That's what God is like!

SCRIPTURE

O sing to the LORD a new song, for [God] has done marvelous things (Psalm 98:1).

Craft

Scherenschnitte (sher-en-shnit) Valentine

Scherenschnitte means "paper cutting." It is an old craft that comes from Europe, especially Poland and Germany. Many Scherenschnitte are very intricate. This design will make a pretty valentine or window hanging for your room.

Fold a 4-inch square of paper in half. Trace the pattern below or create a pattern of your own along the folded edge of the paper. Begin by cutting the outside edge of the image, and then cut out the areas indicated in blue. Open the paper to reveal your design.

fold→

MISSION AROUND THE WORLD

Hungary

Have you heard of Gypsies? Did you know that the people who used to be called Gypsies are actually the Roma? Gypsy was a degrading name given to the Roma a long time ago. Some pictures and stories about Gypsies make us think their lives are happy and carefree—that they travel around dancing and singing. But their lives are not always happy and fun. Often they live without enough food, basic health care, access to education, and shelter. It is estimated that about five million Roma live in Europe, with one to two million in Hungary alone. Other people treat the Roma badly and say that they are dishonest and lazy. But God is doing marvelous things for the Roma in Hungary.

The ground-breaking ceremony for the first church building for a Roma congregation of the Reformed Church of Hungary was held on November 8, 2002. The church is in a small village called Hosszupalyi, about 135 miles east of Budapest. This building will provide a place for all the Roma villagers not only to worship but also to have other community gatherings and cultural events. Find Hungary on the map on page 110.

Mission co-workers Kaeja and Stephen Cho work with Roma families.

PRAYER

God, you make a place of hope for all people. We will sing new songs to you, because you have done marvelous things. In Jesus' name. Amen.

What two PC(USA) presbyteries have partnerships with the Reformed Church in Hungary (RCH)? Look in the Mission Yearbook for Prayer & Study *on the page about Hungary. On the left side of the page are three groups of people to pray for. Find the two partnerships in one of those groups.*

Giving What You Have

In Sunland Park, New Mexico, and in Hungary, a house and a church give new hope for mission work. Put 10 cents into the church offering plate for every room in your home.

What You Can Do

Make a Scherrenschnitte valentine to send to someone in your church. Ask your pastor or church school teacher to help you find a name and address of a person who would like to receive a valentine.

MISSION IN THE UNITED STATES

Presbytery de Cristo

Arizona, New Mexico

Look for the Presbytery de Cristo on the map on page 112 along the border of Mexico. You may have heard about people from Mexico illegally crossing the border into the United States. They are looking for jobs and a better life. But the government of our country wants to limit immigration for many reasons. The government has built walls across traditional migration routes in urban areas and put soldiers along the border, making it more and more difficult for people to cross. Now people try to cross the border through the most desolate and hazardous areas of the Sonoran Desert. Many have risked their lives, dying from lack of water and exposure to the heat in summer or the cold in winter. Since 1998, about 3,500 Mexican people have died trying to cross the border.

Many churches are trying to find ways to save as many lives as possible. Several congregations support a project called Humane Borders. In this project, people set up water stations in the desert along the routes of the migrants. Several congregations work with a group called Samaritans who travel in four-wheel vehicles to help rescue those people who did not prepare properly for the harsh conditions of crossing the desert.

Another project, Just Coffee, lets coffee growers in Chiapas, Mexico, sell their coffee at a fair price and then have it shipped to Agua Prieta in Sonora. There the coffee is roasted and packaged by folks who have come north seeking work. The coffee is sold to many congregations throughout the United States. This way, many farmers can stay on their land and support their families, rather than risk crossing a dangerous border.

Dark, rich coffee beans are grown in Mexico.

SCRIPTURE

You, O Lord, are good and forgiving, abounding in steadfast love to all who call on you (Psalm 86:5).

Recipe

Mexican Coffee

Here is a treat you may help make when there is a party at your house. You should ask for help whenever you use hot water on the stove.

Ingredients

1 qt. whole milk
1 tsp. ground cinnamon
1 tsp. vanilla extract
2/3 cup instant cocoa mix
8 cups boiling water
1/3 cup instant coffee granules (optional)
whipped cream

Combine first 3 ingredients in a Dutch oven or other large pot with a lid. Cook over medium heat until thoroughly heated, but do not allow to boil. Stir in instant cocoa mix. In a large bowl, slowly combine boiling water and coffee granules; stir into milk mixture. Serve with a scoop of whipped cream and, if desired, serve with cinnamon sticks. Makes 3 quarts.

Did You Know?

The Presbyterian Church (U.S.A.) cosponsors the Presbyterian Coffee Project with Equal Exchange, a fair trade company that is owned by the people who work there and that buys 100 percent of its coffees and teas according to fair trade standards. Fair trade means that farmers earn a fair share of income, have access to services that are otherwise unavailable, and get trading partners they can trust.

MISSION AROUND THE WORLD

Ireland

Northern Ireland has been a place of deep divisions for years and years. (Find it on the map on page 110.) The divisions between two groups of people with different religious and political beliefs have caused much hatred and violence. Agnes lives in Belfast, Northern Ireland, one of the cities where the fighting has been bitter. Like others in her group, she would get angry when she saw someone from the other group or heard about them on television. Then in November 2002, she attended a special church service about forgiveness. It was part of a series of services about how the two fighting groups could get over their differences and become friends. The speaker encouraged people to let go of their hatred, hurt, and bitterness by writing a message to God on a sticky note and putting it on a cross in the church. On her note Agnes asked God to help her with her anger toward the other group. The next evening, as she and a friend were leaving the service, she saw a member of the other group on the street. Agnes walked over to him and instead of offering him a fist, offered an open hand and a warm welcome. As she looked into his eyes, she was surprised to see that his eyes were "soft and human." Agnes recognized God's presence in this meeting. God had answered her prayer for help and given her strength to live out Jesus' command to love one another.

PRAYER

Think about someone in your life that you sometimes feel anger toward. Ask God to help you learn how to forgive. Write down on a sticky note (or a piece of paper with tape) how you want God to help you. Tape it somewhere in your room so you can see it.

Giving What You Have

Sometime two of your friends may have a disagreement. See if you can help by being a good listener to each and give them a chance to learn by your example.

Forgiving

People are often divided by many types of borders and walls! Forgiving as God forgives can be difficult, but it helps us break down the barriers that divide us.

What You Can Do

Find out if any immigrants live near you. See if your church school teacher can have an immigrant come to your class or church and talk about what it's like to live in a new country.

SCRIPTURE

If then there is any encouragement, . . . any sharing in the Spirit, . . . make my joy complete: be of the same mind, having the same love, being in full accord and of one mind (Philippians 2:1–2).

Giving What You Have

See if you can discover how many Presbyterian churches are in your neighborhood or city. Give 5 cents for each one to your church on Sunday.

Word Puzzle: Twenty-six Ways to Say Help

Find and circle the 26 synonyms for "help" in the puzzle. Words can go up, down, backward, and diagonal. When you are finished, you will see the 4-word mystery phrase in letters not circled in the first 3 lines. Hint: Some letters are used more than once.

N	T	R	G	O	D	I	B	E	S	A	E	L	P	C
O	E	N	E	S	O	U	R	E	S	T	O	R	E	O
I	A	R	E	C	H	E	L	P	F	H	A	N	D	M
T	C	W	R	M	O	M	L	A	B	R	I	V	Z	F
A	H	B	O	U	E	G	E	E	D	A	I	B	H	O
R	I	G	P	R	R	V	N	W	G	H	I	E	Y	R
E	N	Z	T	E	D	C	O	I	V	N	A	O	N	T
P	G	E	E	I	O	Z	B	R	T	L	L	K	H	D
O	Y	H	C	U	F	L	C	E	P	I	P	N	S	Z
O	C	I	R	N	E	E	R	V	G	M	O	X	I	R
C	R	A	I	S	A	E	N	H	V	S	I	N	R	E
M	G	R	S	V	S	D	T	E	S	H	E	N	U	T
E	P	I	C	T	N	E	I	E	B	A	X	L	O	T
P	N	G	E	J	N	A	L	U	S	K	O	A	N	E
G	E	T	O	M	O	R	P	E	G	E	V	A	S	B

Mystery Phrase: __ __ __ __ __ __ __ __ __ __ __ __ __ __

BALM	COMFORT	GUIDANCE	LESSON	RECOGNITION
BEFRIEND	COOPERATION	HAND	LIGHTEN	RESTORE
BENEFIT	EASE	HEAL	NOURISH	SAVE
BETTER	ENCOURAGE	IMPROVEMENT	PLEASE	TEACHING
BLESSING	GAIN	INTEREST	PROMOTE	WORD
CHEER				

MISSION IN THE UNITED STATES
Presbytery of Grand Canyon
Arizona

The people of the Presbytery of Grand Canyon, along with numerous winter visitors, show God's love for people in many ways. At one of two new church developments in the presbytery, members sell African beadwork to support Nasaru Ntoyie, which means "Save the Girls." This organization in Kenya rescues young girls from parents intent on selling or trading them in marriage. Several churches take turns giving temporary lodging for homeless families for one week every three months. A team of thirty volunteers from Orangewood Presbyterian Church in Phoenix makes an annual trek to Rocky Point, Mexico, to build two-room houses at a cost of $3,000 each. Members of First Presbyterian Church in Mesa formed Christ Haven to assist people in need with food, housing, and utilities. Northminster Presbyterian Church in Phoenix adopts foster care group homes to provide emotional and spiritual help to children who are alone in the world. Find this presbytery on the map on page 112.

Presbytery of Grand Canyon members sell African beadwork to support Nasaru Ntoyie.

Did You Know?

"Bisa bantu saya?" means "Can you help me?" in Bahasa Indonesia.
"Please, can you help me?" in Mandarin is "Qing wen ni ke yi bang wo yi ge mang ma?"

Encouragement

Word of the Week

As Christians, we encourage each other with missions, unity, kind words, prayers, smiles, and friendship.

PRAYER

God, we are many people, different and diverse. Help us to be one, having one mind together, the mind of your love and care. Help us to encourage one another. Thank you for the work of the churches in Malaysia and in the Presbytery of Grand Canyon. In Jesus' name. Amen.

MISSION AROUND THE WORLD

Malaysia

Penang is a small island on the western side of the Malay Peninsula. Find the two parts of Malaysia on the map on page 110. The Malay Peninsula is the part of Malaysia that's below Thailand.

The Rev. Dr. Joseph Ong is the pastor of Saint Andrew's Presbyterian Church, the only Presbyterian congregation on the island of Penang. People in the church and on the island are of different ethnic groups and speak different languages. For twenty-five years, Dr. Ong has worked to help the people live together as Christ's disciples despite their differences. Even though St. Andrew's Church conducts two worship services in two languages, Mandarin and English, it is unified as one congregation with one session represented by two elders, one from each language group. Saint Andrew's also reaches out to college students and youth from Indonesia. Once a week the church hosts a youth worship service in Bahasa Indonesia, the language of Indonesia. Church members hope to raise up new young leaders in the church.

This Sunday: Services in **BAHASA MANDARIN INDONESIA ENGLISH**

What You Can Do

Everyone needs some encouragement now and then. Make a phone call or write a note of encouragement to someone in your church, your family, or a neighbor.

keep the faith!

MISSION IN THE UNITED STATES
Presbytery of San Gabriel
California

Talk about choices! In the Presbytery of San Gabriel, each weekend (take a deep breath!) 6 groups worship in Spanish, 6 in Korean, 2 in Arabic, 5 in Taiwanese, 2 in Cantonese, 1 in Mandarin, 1 in Farsi, 1 in Indonesian, 1 in Thai, and 40 in English—with a little bit of Tagalog and Japanese sprinkled in! Have you added up the number of choices? We count 65—40 services in English and 25 in other languages! That is a lot to celebrate!

Twenty percent of the members in the churches have Asian last names. The presbytery gets a lot of help from the Asian Presbyterian Council of the synod. They work hard to find ministers and leaders who understand these 12 languages and cultures. They trust God to show them new ways to love all kinds of people. Find the Presbytery of San Gabriel on the map on page 112.

Giving What You Have

How many languages are spoken in your church? For the language most people speak, put 25 cents into the offering plate on Sunday. Add 10 cents more for each additional language you know about.

SCRIPTURE

For God's foolishness is wiser than human wisdom, and God's weakness is stronger than human strength (1 Corinthians 1:25).

Craft
Loy Krathong Floating Light

In Thailand, people celebrate a festival called Loy Krathong. Every autumn, they set little floating lights into the river. The lights are made of lotus leaves decorated with flowers and a tiny candle.

Materials

flat piece of Styrofoam, about 5" square
permanent markers
small flowers, real or silk
leaves, real or silk
tea light candle
glue that doesn't wash off (craft glue)

Decorate the Styrofoam with the markers. You may want to cut it into a leaf shape. Glue the candle down in the center of the Styrofoam, then glue the flowers and leaves around it. Be sure that silk leaves and flowers will not be near the flame of the candle. When you have finished, get an adult to help you light the candle and float it in a large bowl!

What You Can Do

Work with your friends at church to create a drama or dance that tells a Bible story. Ask your pastor or teacher when you can share it with others.

MISSION AROUND THE WORLD

Thailand

How long has it been since 1828? That's the year the Church of Christ in Thailand (CCT) counts as its first year! The CCT includes churches that were started by Baptist, Disciples of Christ, and Presbyterian missionaries. Our mission co-workers, Robert Collins and Esther Wakeman (they are married to each other, even though they do not have the same last name), both work in Chiang-Mai at Payap University, a CCT school. Esther works in the Department of Religious Affairs there; and Robert is in charge of the Christian Communication Institute, which was founded about twenty years ago by a Broadway star who became a mission worker to Thailand. The institute uses traditional and modern drama and music to present the gospel in schools and villages all over Thailand.

Find Thailand on the map on page 110.

The Christian Communication Institute brings Bible stories to life using traditional Thai dance and drama.

PRAYER

God, sometimes when we think we are wise, we are not. But you are always wise. Thank you for giving wisdom to the churches in the Presbytery of San Gabriel. Thank you for the creative people of the Church of Christ in Thailand. Teach us your wisdom. In Jesus' name. Amen.

Activity

Just as the Christian Communication Institute in Thailand uses music and drama to present the gospel, we can express thanks to God in ways other than words. Psalm 111:1 says, "I will give thanks to the LORD with my whole heart." How can you use your whole body to show your thanks to God? Try turning, jumping, balancing on one foot, running, skipping, falling, and sliding. Can you feel your body being thankful?

Did You Know?

The country of Thailand was called Siam until 1939. The word *Thai* means "free."

Word of the Week — Wisdom

Wisdom is what helps us make good and thoughtful choices. Wisdom helps us choose the way that brings the most good.

MISSION IN THE UNITED STATES

Presbytery of the Pacific

California, Hawaii

Lucy Cortez is a member at Immanuel Presbyterian Church. She came to Los Angeles from El Salvador fifteen years ago. Lucy worked hard to create a good home life for her children. But she faced some problems. One of her biggest problems was that she did not have any health insurance. It was hard to get the kind of health care her children needed. Sometimes they had to wait a long time to see a doctor, and sometimes they could not find anyone to help them. So Lucy went to Health Rescue, a place where she could learn how to be a community health promoter. After she finished her training, she wanted to have a health fair for the whole community in the church's parking lot. A health fair is a way for people to find out about services and information they need to stay healthy. Lucy's church worked with Health Rescue to create a health fair. On a sunny summer Saturday, over 500 children and adults went to the health fair. Children received vaccines and parents learned more about health issues like diabetes, dental care, and cancer prevention. Best of all, it was a wonderful way for the church to share in God's ministry of healing in its community.

Find the Presbytery of the Pacific on the map on page 112.

SCRIPTURE

"And these are the ones sown on the good soil: they hear the word and accept it and bear fruit" (Mark 4:20).

Recipe

Thit Nuong Cha (Vietnamese Meatballs)

Makes about 25 meatballs
Reminder: Wash your hands well after handling raw meat.

Ingredients

1 1/2 pounds ground turkey, beef, or pork
1/2 onion, chopped fine
1/2 tsp. fish sauce or Worcestershire sauce
2 tsp. tamari or soy sauce
1/2 tsp. pepper
1/2 tsp. sugar
1/4 tsp. salt
1/4 tsp. dry mustard
2 tbs. bread crumbs
2 tbs. finely chopped parsley

Preheat oven to 300°F. Put everything in a large mixing bowl and mix well. The easiest way to do it is to squish everything together with your hands. Roll the meat mixture into one-inch balls. Place in a baking dish and set on counter for 20 minutes. Bake uncovered for 30 minutes. Make sure that the meatballs are cooked all the way through! Serve with sauce for dipping. You can use soy sauce, fish sauce, sweet and sour sauce, or Worcestershire sauce.

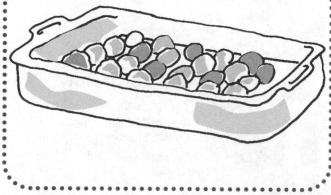

MISSION AROUND THE WORLD

Vietnam

Binh Nguyen grew up in Vietnam. (Can you find Vietnam on the map on page 110?) That's where he met his wife, Chau. They left Vietnam soon after the communist government took over in 1975. Binh and Chau came to the United States. They are members at Mercer Island Presbyterian Church. Binh is a commissioned lay pastor in the PC(USA). (If you don't know what that is, take a look at Did You Know on this page.)

When Mercer Island Church decided to send a group of members to Vietnam, Binh and Chau were invited to go along. Binh says he remembers praying, "God, I know you aren't sending me back to be a tourist."

While they were in Vietnam, Binh met some Christian people who were having church meetings in their homes. The people of Mercer Island Church had been helping people in Vietnam for a long time. Now they wanted to help the "house churches." With the help of many people in Vietnam and the United States, those house churches became the Vietnam Presbyterian Church!

Mercer Island Presbyterian Church representatives meet with members of a house church in Vietnam.

Word of the Week — Hear

When Jesus told us to "hear," he meant we should really listen and then do something. In the stories for this week, Lucy and Binh heard the good news, really listened, and then acted!

PRAYER

God, help me to hear your message and do your work. Help me to share your love. Bless all those who hear and do your word, especially Lucy in the Presbytery of the Pacific and Binh and the new churches of Vietnam. In Jesus' name. Amen.

Did You Know?

A commissioned lay pastor (CLP) is an elder who is trained and commissioned by the presbytery to do the kinds of things pastors normally do in churches that don't have pastors.

Sometimes they serve in a group of churches as part of ministry teams, and sometimes they serve as part-time pastors of small churches. They can work with new immigrant populations, churches who are seeking an ordained pastor, new church developments, and redeveloping churches.

Giving What You Have

How many people who work in health care do you know? Count them up and for each one give 5 cents to your church on Sunday.

What You Can Do

When you hear the good news of God's love, you can act, too! Lucy and Binh used their special gifts to help others. What special gifts can you bring to your church? Ask God to help you hear and act!

MISSION IN THE UNITED STATES

Presbytery of Riverside
California

H ave you learned estimating skills in school? Let's estimate this: In the region of the Presbytery of Riverside, there are 3.3 million people. About 35 percent of the people are Hispanic, which is a little more than one-third. About how many of the 3.3 million are Hispanic? If your estimate is about 1.1 million, you are a good estimator! Many Taiwanese, Korean, Indonesian, Native American, and Urdu-speaking Pakistani and Indian people also live in the area.

Because of all the many different kinds of people, the churches are becoming different in new and exciting ways. First Presbyterian Church of Colton used to be struggling because it had fewer and fewer members. Now it is growing and becoming a multicultural church with Indonesian and Hispanic people. Westminster Presbyterian Church in Ontario started a Spanish-speaking ministry to go along with its English-speaking ministry. The church has Spanish-speaking and English-speaking co-pastors. It would be hard to estimate how much God's love is building up the many different people in the presbytery!

Find the Presbytery of Riverside on the map on page 112.

SCRIPTURE

Knowledge puffs up, but love builds up (1 Corinthians 8:1).

Word Puzzle: Falling Tiles

The letters are lined up under the column where they belong, but they have fallen out of place. Return the letters to the correct rows to see Jesus' command for putting love into action. Hint: Start with shorter words. Stumped? Look up Matthew 28:19a.

MISSION AROUND THE WORLD

Pakistan

Thirty-two years ago, the government of Pakistan took over Forman Christian College in Lahore. Last year, the college was returned to the Christian community. It took leaders nine years to work all this out. The college will need to find lots of help. They will need new teachers and money to fix things up. But they are excited and hopeful that the PC(USA) can once again share God's love through teaching and learning at Forman Christian College. The president of Pakistan, Pervez Musharraf, is a graduate of Forman Christian College. Presbyterians also support a literacy program for children at the St. Thomas Church in Islamabad, Pakistan, where children prepare for going to school. Find Pakistan on the map on page 110.

Children learn numbers in the literacy program of St. Thomas Church in Islamabad.

PRAYER

God, we see your love in action in Pakistan and in the Presbytery of Riverside. Help us to be your love in action, wherever we are. In Jesus' name. Amen.

Did You Know?

Urdu is an official language spoken in Pakistan. "God loves you" is said this way in Urdu: "Aap Khuda sai muhabbat" (you God loves).

Khuda	muhabbat	aap
God	**loves**	**you**

The Mission Yearbook for Prayer & Study gives us the names of mission workers who served at least twenty years overseas and who are now retired. Find six retired mission workers who served in Pakistan on page 375 in Appendix C. Hint: The countries where mission workers served are in parentheses after their names. If you are feeling energetic, see how many more people worked in Pakistan by looking on the pages following 375.

Giving What You Have

How many schools have the people in your family attended? Don't forget to ask the grown-ups. Save 5 cents for each school to put in the One Great Hour of Sharing Offering, which most churches will receive on Easter.

Word of the Week

Love

Love is a noun and a verb. A verb is an action word! Mission puts God's love in action.

What You Can Do

Find out what your church does to support schools and colleges in other countries. Let your friends and family know how they can help.

MISSION IN THE UNITED STATES

Flint River Presbytery

Georgia

Fifty-four churches, all with different gifts. Fifty-four congregations challenged to pray, study, and talk—and then to start one new mission project to meet the needs of their community. That's the new challenge that Flint River Presbytery faces! But many congregations are already doing good work in missions.

The presbytery has adopted Covenant Hospital at Mombin Crochu, Haiti. Several churches have sent work and medical teams to the hospital. One church sent an ambulance! They send money to help support the salaries of Paul and Joan McClain, medical mission workers in Haiti. They also have pledged to raise $100,000 toward a new airplane that is being designed to transport and support mission workers. The presbytery writes to say, "We know we are among the blessed, and we remember Jesus' words—those who have been given much, of them much will be required. We now recommit ourselves to fulfilling our Lord's commandment this year." Find this presbytery on the map on page 112.

Children play in front of Covenant Hospital in Mombin Crochu, Haiti.

photo by the Rev. Barry Ferguson

SCRIPTURE

Now there are varieties of gifts, but the same Spirit (1 Corinthians 12:4).

Craft

Batik Table Runner

Batik is an Indonesian way of decorating cloth. In real batik, hot wax is put onto the fabric to make a design. Then the cloth is dyed and the wax is scraped off. The places where there was wax stay white, while the rest of the cloth is colored. You can make a "batik" table runner for your home or church.

Materials

15" x 36" strip of white cloth, either plain muslin or cotton (You can use an old sheet.)
white school glue (the kind that washes out)
cold spray dye (You can buy a mix and put it in a spray bottle, or you can find the spray dye in the craft store.)

Find a place to spread your fabric out. Outside is best. If you are working inside, use a table or the floor. Be sure to cover your workspace with newspapers to protect the floor or table. Draw the designs on your cloth with the glue. Simple designs and shapes like circles, spirals, dots, or stars will work best. Let the glue dry, then spray the colors on. Use one, two, or three colors. When the dye is dry, wash the cloth according to the instructions on the spray dye or mix. The glue will wash out and your design will show up in white!

MISSION AROUND THE WORLD

Indonesia

Farsijana Adeney-Risakotta was appointed a mission co-worker with the PC(USA) in January 2003. Her husband, Bernard Adeney-Risakotta, has been a mission worker for more than eleven years. They are faculty members at Duta Wacana Christian University in Yogyakarta, on the island of Java in Indonesia. Find Indonesia on the map on page 110. Farsijana writes about Easter 2003. She and Bernie met with twenty-five Muslims and twenty-five Christians from the Moluccas, an island group in the far western part of Indonesia. This was the first major meeting between Christians and Muslims since an outbreak of violence in early 1999. "We came together in our home and shared food, prayers, songs, poems, and thoughts. They planned some activities to help clear suspicions and break down the barriers of fear between people that resulted from civil war." The Muslims and Christians were happy to have this time of friendship after years of violence and distrust.

PRAYER

This week be aware of when someone uses their gifts for others. Thank God for that person and the gift. As you share your gifts with others this week, thank God for the gifts God has given you.

Did You Know?

Indonesia has been in the news lately because of fighting that has happened there. But the country of Indonesia has wonderful gifts! Orchids grow there. Nutmeg comes from the Moluccas. Weaving, shadow puppets, and beautiful batik fabrics all come from Indonesia.

Word of the Week — Gifts

God has given us so many gifts! And each of us has gifts to share with our church and our community. What can you give as a gift to your community, your family, and your church?

Giving What You Have

What are your gifts? Are you good at music? Telling jokes? Laughing? Spelling? Make a list of all your gifts, and share them with others this week.

What You Can Do

Look around you this week and see all the gifted people you know! Some people are gifted with words, some with art, some with cooking, some with being loving and kind. But everyone is gifted. Tell the gifted people you know how glad you are to know them.

Word of the Week

Hospitality

Hospitality means giving guests a generous welcome, but it also means creating a pleasant or supportive environment. God's word calls us to hospitality—in both ways!

MISSION IN THE UNITED STATES

Presbytery of St. Augustine

Florida

Have you ever heard someone say, "Getting that job done was like pulling teeth"? For Dr. Jim Gaff, getting the job done *was* pulling teeth! Dr. Gaff is a dentist who went to Jamaica with 28 other medical workers as part of the Jamaica Ecumenical Mission. The Presbytery of St. Augustine has a partnership with Jamaica Ecumenical Mission, and Dr. Gaff makes regular trips to Jamaica as a part of the medical mission.

On his last trip, people lined up early to receive the only medical attention that they might get for several years. When it was their turn, patients would tell the doctor what tooth was bothering them. Some had as few as 12 remaining "good" teeth to choose from. With a wad of gauze to bite down on and a small packet of painkiller in hand, each patient left the area with a nod of appreciation to the doctor. In 6 long days 2 dentists saw 333 patients, pulled 521 teeth, replaced 68 teeth, and performed 6 root canals. Sometimes hospitality may mean pulling teeth!

Find the Presbytery of St. Augustine on the map on page 112.

SCRIPTURE

"Whoever welcomes one such child in my name welcomes me, and whoever welcomes me welcomes not me but the one who sent me" (Mark 9:37).

Giving What You Have

How many teeth have you lost so far? Instead of putting something under your pillow, save a quarter for each tooth you have lost to put in the One Great Hour of Sharing Offering.

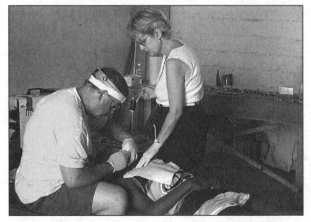

Dr. Jim Gaff is assisted by Barbara Heimer in providing dental work to a patient in Patrick Town, Jamaica.

Find where the Scripture verse that appears this week in this book is also used in the Mission Yearbook for Prayer & Study. Hint: It will be on a page in the week of March 28–April 3.

What You Can Do

Ask your parents or church school teachers to help you collect toothbrushes and toothpaste to take to a shelter for homeless people in your area.

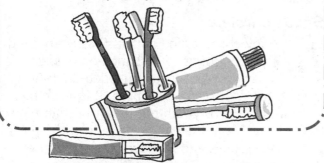

Recipe

Pisang Goreng (Fried Bananas)

This is a favorite dessert in Singapore and Indonesia! Try this easy version. Note: this is definitely a recipe you should do with an adult—frying can be tricky!

Ingredients

4 bananas
1 cup biscuit mix
1/2 cup coconut milk
1/2 cup cooking oil

Stir the biscuit mix with the coconut milk to make a smooth batter. It should be a little thicker than pancake batter. If it is too thick, stir in a little water. Peel the bananas and slice them lengthwise, so that they look like "banana planks." Heat the oil in a deep, heavy skillet until it is very hot but not smoking. Dip the banana pieces in the batter, let the excess drip off, then fry on both sides until golden brown. Sprinkle with powdered sugar. Yum!

PRAYER

Welcoming God, you love and support all people. Even in the hospitality of pulling teeth, we see your love! Bless the people of the Presbytery of St. Augustine and of Singapore. Teach us to be generous and welcoming too. In Jesus' name. Amen.

MISSION AROUND THE WORLD

Singapore

Christ gave his disciples a new commandment to love one another even as he had loved them (John 13:34). For many years, the Presbyterian Church of Singapore has loved others through service to the community. One way the church serves is through Care Corner Singapore. In the Chinese-speaking community, people struggle with little money, little education, and a language barrier. Care Corner helps them by providing counseling, child care, elderly care, and family support. What began as a hotline counseling service in 1981 has grown into 23 centers. There are 3 centers for the elderly, 4 family service centers, 5 student care centers, a Chinese child care center, a youth club, and an academic counseling center to aid students preparing for their college entry examinations. The aim is to serve, strengthen, and support families, because strong, stable families are the foundation upon which community is built. Find Singapore on the map on page 110.

Did You Know?

Singapore means "Lion City." Legend has it that in the thirteenth century Prince Sang Nila Utama was shipwrecked on the shores of an island and saw a strange creature. He was impressed by the majestic appearance of the creature and asked for its name. The local fishermen told him that it was a lion. The prince then gave the island the name Singa Pura (which means "Lion City").

SCRIPTURE

My help comes from the LORD, who made heaven and earth (Psalm 121:2).

Giving What You Have

How many verses are there in Psalm 121? Read it and save 10 cents for each verse to put in the One Great Hour of Sharing Offering.

MISSION IN THE UNITED STATES

Foothills Presbytery

South Carolina

Many churches in Foothills Presbytery send youth groups to do hands-on mission work where they are needed. In 1986 the Foothills Workcamp was born. It is a summer program that helps youth put their Christian faith to work and share their love and faith with others. They make repairs and improvements to houses of elderly people and others without resources. They help people to live in clean, safe, comfortable surroundings. They also work with people who are homeless and with food banks, clothes closets, and vacation Bible schools. Youth from Foothills Presbytery went to Florida to work in the Duvall Presbyterian Home for adults and children with developmental disablities. They played games and spent time with the residents. Find Foothills Presbytery on the map on page 112.

Youth work at the Duvall Presbyterian Home.

Word Puzzle

Missing Vowels

All the vowels in this sentence are missing! Can you find them and put them back where they belong? Vowels are A E I O U and sometimes Y.

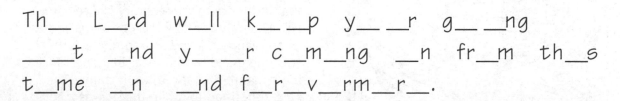

```
Th__ L__rd w__ll k____p y____r g____ng
____t __nd y____r c__m__ng __n fr__m th__s
t__me __n __nd f__r__v__rm__r__.
```

Hint: the answer is in the last verse of Psalm 121.

What You Can Do

You may not yet be old enough to join the youth group in your church. But you and others your age can help your youth group when they are raising funds for mission trips and mission work. Ask the youth leader or the pastor what you and your friends can do to help out. Remember, someday it will be YOU who is working to raise money for a mission trip!

Did You Know?

In 1989 the military government changed the name of Burma to Myanmar. One of the earliest mission workers to Myanmar (then called Burma) was a Presbyterian named Daniel McGilvary. It is said that he and his co-workers rode elephants from Thailand to bring the good news to the Dai people.

Word of the Week

Assurance

Assurance is knowing you can count on something or someone. We have assurance that we can trust God. The words of Psalm 121 give us assurance of God's care.

PRAYER

We have assurance from you, O God, that you will help us. As you watch over us, we know that you will keep the Dai people in your care as well. God, make us ready to grow up to be mission workers, like the youth groups of Foothills Presbytery, so that wherever we go and whatever work we do, we will share with others the assurance of your love. In Jesus' name. Amen.

MISSION AROUND THE WORLD

Myanmar

Myanmar is near China. Find it on the map on page 110. The Dai people live in the mountains of southern Chin State in western Myanmar. They are a very isolated people. The gospel was first brought to them through the work of a mission worker from the Presbyterian Church of Myanmar (PCM). His name was Upa (which means "elder") C. Bukchhuaka. At that time, communities sometimes didn't take very good care of little children who had no parents. Upa Bukchhuaka found many babies and children who had no one to take care of them. He began an orphanage and gradually encouraged communities to take better care of the children. Thanks to his efforts and those of other PCM mission workers who followed, Christianity was established among the Dai. The PCM is almost 50 years old. It now has 30,000 members in over 250 congregations.

One Great Hour of Sharing

MISSION IN THE UNITED STATES

Charleston-Atlantic Presbytery

About fifteen years ago, a very large and powerful hurricane named Hurricane Hugo crossed over southeastern United States and did a great deal of damage to states on the coasts along both the Atlantic Ocean and the Gulf of Mexico. One of the first places it hit while it was at its strongest was the South Carolina coast. An island near Charleston called Sullivan's Island was one of the hardest hit areas. Most of the homes were expensive, and the people who lived in them were not used to needing help from other people. But people came from all over to help them repair the damages. They worked with Presbyterian Disaster Assistance, a program supported by gifts to One Great Hour of Sharing. Presbyterian Disaster Assistance helped organize the volunteers. The people of Sullivan's Island learned that sometimes it's as difficult to accept help as it is to be willing to give it.

Several years later, another powerful hurricane, Hurricane Andrew, crashed into the Atlantic coast hundreds of miles away near Homestead, Florida. Among the people who showed up first to help were a number of people from Sullivan's Island. They had learned how wonderful it can be to have people helping them face the nightmare of losing much of what they took for granted.

Word of the Week

Sangham

This is a word from India that means a cooperative, a way for people who don't have much money to make themselves stronger by working together. The women in the Mission Around the World story formed a sangham.

SCRIPTURE

One of his disciples, Andrew, Simon Peter's brother, said to him, "There is a boy here who has five barley loaves and two fish. But what are they among so many people?" (John 6:8–9).

What You Can Do

One of the ways guests were welcomed into a home in the time of Jesus was to have their feet washed. The roads were dusty, and after a journey people's feet were bound to be pretty dirty! But because washing someone's feet was such a dirty job, it was usually done by a servant. During the last supper that Jesus shared with his disciples before he was arrested and crucified, he chose to wash the feet of his disciples. You can imagine how surprised they were! He was their leader and teacher, and here he was doing the task of one of the lowliest of household servants. He told them that this was an example for them to follow.

Try this with your church school class or with members of your own family: Ask them if you can wash their feet. Partly fill a pan with lukewarm water and bring a washcloth and towel. Take off the first person's shoes and socks and gently wash that person's feet with the damp washcloth. Dry the feet with the towel. Ask the person if he or she wants the shoes back on. If so, put the shoes on for the person before you move on to the next person. Remember as you are doing this that it is a way of showing them respect and love, and that it is how Jesus showed the disciples that being willing to do the humblest task is part of what it takes to follow Jesus.

Giving What You Have

Every day this week, think of one thing you like to do, like getting an ice cream cone, going to the movies, getting a fast-food meal, getting a CD of your favorite group, or buying a soft drink. Choose one or two of these things, estimate how much they cost, and put that amount of money in your One Great Hour of Sharing coin bank. If you don't have a bank, save the money and put it in an offering envelope the day your congregation receives the offering.

Did You Know?

One Great Hour of Sharing was started fifty-five years ago when Christians in this country decided they needed to find ways to help people in Europe and Asia recover from the damages of World War II. They did a one-hour nationwide radio broadcast with several major stars and even President Harry Truman asking people to give the next day in their churches. The response convinced them to repeat the offering the next year. Since then it has become a yearly tradition in many denominations like the United Methodist Church, the United Church of Christ, and the Presbyterian Church (U.S.A.).

PRAYER

God, we know that you are the Creator of everything we have and everything we are. We believe that giving is one of the ways you show your love for us and that when we share with one another, it is a way of extending that love. We sometimes think that what we have to give can make very little difference in anyone else's life. Help us to remember that what you can do with our gifts is beyond what we can imagine and that when we give any gift in love, you can work miracles with it. In Jesus' name we pray. Amen.

MISSION AROUND THE WORLD

India

Dalits is the name given to a group in India formerly known as the untouchables. They did many of the jobs regarded as unclean and were shunned by other people. They had few opportunities to earn much money at all and so were very poor.

In Vazhkudai (VOZH koo die), a village in southern India, a group of women decided that they had some skills, and if they organized themselves, they could use those skills to make a better future for their families. They knew how to take care of cows, and with a grant from Self-Development of People (one of the programs supported by One Great Hour of Sharing), they were able to buy a cow for each household. They got training in how to make the cows healthier so they would give more milk. Now the cows produce at least twice as much milk as they did before, which means the women not only have enough for their families but also can sell what's left over to earn money. Find India on the map on page 110.

Girls in Vazhkudai learn early how to take care of cows.

MISSION IN THE UNITED STATES

Presbytery of Denver

Colorado

For 117 years the little white church in Elbert, Colorado, served God and the community. For a while the church was a blend of Presbyterians and other denominations. Now the church in Elbert is Presbyterian again and has a new pastor. New members have come, and they are welcomed by the old members. Elbert Presbyterian Church has become "the little church that could"! New offerings, like musical programs, dinners, and trail rides have meant more new people! The church also received some money from a Colorado State Historical Fund

Elbert Presbyterian Church is "the little church that can."

grant, which will help to restore the church building to its original 1885 appearance. More changes are coming. Elbert County is among the ten fastest growing counties in the nation. As more new people come to Elbert, the church will be praying that God will help them continue to be "the little church that can"! Find the Presbytery of Denver on the map on page 112.

SCRIPTURE

Peace I leave with you; my peace I give to you (John 14:27).

Craft

Often in the Himalayan Mountains, climbers are helped by Sherpas, native people who live in the mountains of Nepal. Many Sherpa people are Buddhist, and they display prayer flags. You can make a set of prayer flags using Christian symbols.

Materials

yellow, green, red, white, and blue
    tissue paper
6 feet of yarn or cord
black paint or black marker
tape

Cut one sheet of each color, 12 inches wide and 15 inches long. Paint or draw a Christian symbol on each one: a cross, a dove, a shell, a crown, and a star. Tape yarn to the top two corners of each sheet of tissue paper. Tie the ends of the yarn so that the flags are all in a row, fluttering in the breeze.

MISSION AROUND THE WORLD

Nepal

The Kingdom of Nepal is a diverse land. Find Nepal on the map on page 110. In the south the land is fairly low and can be farmed. There are forests, and then the land rises to form the main section of the Himalayas in the north, including Mt. Everest, the world's highest peak. Nepal is one of the poorest countries in the region. The annual Thank Offering (including Health Ministries) of Presbyterian Women helps support projects that provide hope. One of these projects is in Janakpur, close to the border with India. Many

families in this area are tenants on farms. That means they do not own the land they farm, and they only get to keep half of what they raise. The program gives farm animals and plants to women. With their very own animals and plants, the women can have a little extra income and a little extra food.

Millet is one of the crops grown on farms in Nepal.

Word of the Week

Peace

In many Presbyterian churches, we "pass the peace" of Christ each week. The peace Christ gives us is within us and lasts forever.

Find out what kind of organization (and its name) in Nepal has the nickname "light on the hill" and the motto "We Serve, Jesus Heals," and why people as far away as India go there. The answer is in the Mission Yearbook for Prayer & Study on the second page about Nepal.

PRAYER

Thank you, God, for the work of your people in Nepal and in Elbert, Colorado. May they and all people know the peace of Christ, in whose name we pray. Amen.

What You Can Do

This week, look for someone who might need to know the peace Christ gives. Perhaps it is someone who is lonely or scared. Take time to tell that person that Jesus loves him or her, and share Christ's peace.

Did You Know?

Many people from Tibet have fled the country and are now refugees living in Nepal. To get to Nepal they have to cross the Himalayan Mountains.

Giving What You Have

Find out about Presbyterian Women in your church. Offer to attend a meeting and share a story with them from the *Children's Mission Yearbook.*

PRESBYTERIAN WOMEN

SCRIPTURE

Cast all your anxiety on [God], because [God] cares for you (1 Peter 5:7).

MISSION IN THE UNITED STATES

Presbytery of Plains and Peaks

Colorado, Nebraska

When you think of "Highlands," do you think of Scotland? Think again, and this time think of the Rocky Mountains. The Highlands Presbyterian Camp and Retreat Center is a great place for Presbyterians to gather. It is in the Presbytery of Plains and Peaks. Find this presbytery on the map on page 112. Highlands recently completed a 30,000-square-foot adult conference facility. This four-season mountain lodge joins other national Presbyterian retreat centers in providing space for conferences, meetings, seminars, and retreats. The center can accommodate over 100 persons with twenty-four motel-style bedrooms with private baths and a dining hall that can be used for meals and for all kinds of meetings. Highlands also offers programs and rustic three-season cabins for all age groups.

Recipe

Platanos (Green Plantain Chips)

This tasty dessert from Honduras made from an angular greenish starchy fruit of the plantain tree (banana tree) is a staple food in the tropics when it's cooked. You'll need an adult to help.

Ingredients

vegetable oil
1 large green plantain
    (about 1 pound)
salt, if desired

Peel skin from the plantain and cut off the strings. Slice the plantain into thin circles. Put 2 or 3 inches of vegetable oil in a large frying pan and heat until a drop of water sizzles. Fry plantain slices until golden brown on both sides (about 3 to 4 minutes). Drain on paper towels. Sprinkle with salt. Serve chips warm or at room temperature. Makes 4 servings.

MISSION AROUND THE WORLD

Honduras

The people of Honduras face lots of problems. (Find Honduras on the map on page 110.) Sometimes it is hard for them to know what to do about their problems. Since 1998, a circle of women has been meeting in the tiny community of Quebrada Honda, in the mountains of western Honduras. They look at the problems in their community and decide which are most important. Then they work together to solve them. The Circle of Friends and Neighbors, as it is called, is growing. It is now an organization of 150 people made up of ten circles—each with its own name. The women now manage a chicken project through Heifer Project International. The chickens and their chicks and eggs are benefiting 98 families. People who receive chickens give the baby chicks to others. Someday maybe everyone in the community will have animals. Best of all, working together makes the circle of friends and neighbors stronger and more caring.

The Circle of Friends and Neighbors provides a sense of community for these women of Honduras.

Word of the Week

Trust

When we trust people, it is because we have faith that we can count on them, based on past experience. That's why we trust God, knowing from all the stories of the past that we can count on God.

PRAYER

Ask your family to make a circle of prayer. Have all the members of your family sit in a circle and ask each one who is willing to name a concern or joy. Offer these to God.

Giving What You Have

There are over 150 retreat and conference centers in the PC(USA). Give one penny for each one in next Sunday's offering.

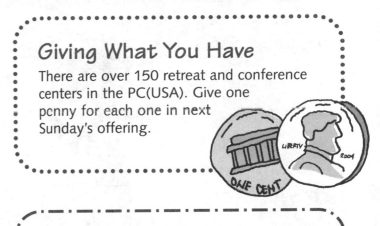

What You Can Do

Are there problems to solve in your community? Form your own circle of friends and neighbors. Decide as a group what is important and then work together to solve the problem.

Did You Know?

The American Sign Language sign for "trust" is very much like the sign for "faith." To sign "trust," hold your hands out, palms facing your body, then shape your hands like you are holding onto a rope. To sign "faith," point to your forehead with your first finger (the sign for "think"), then hold your hands out, palms facing your body, and shape your hands like you are holding onto a rope. (The sign for 'faith" combines the signs "think" and "trust.")

SCRIPTURE

"You are the salt of the earth. . . . You are the light of the world" (Matthew 5:13–14).

Did You Know?

The word *light* is used in 207 verses of the Bible. The word *darkness* is used in 154 verses. Thats about 1/4 more verses about light!

MISSION IN THE UNITED STATES

Presbytery of Wyoming

After their pastor visited Croatia in 1999, members of Shepherd of the Hills Presbyterian Church in Casper became interested in what he told them about the country upon his return. They wanted to visit Croatia themselves. So they studied the history of Croatia, and they took a class about teaching English as a second language. Then six church members traveled to Zagreb, Croatia. In that beautiful city they met a group of young adults who were eager to learn English. The church members taught English classes at the Reformed Christian Church of Croatia Mission Center. For practice, they went to a nearby coffeehouse and had conversations in English with the students. Shepherd of the Hills also supports the Presbyterian Church of Pine Ridge, South Dakota. Four times a year, they take several carloads of children's clothing, groceries, and other supplies to people who need them. They are God's light in their home state and around the world.

Shepherd of the Hills Presbyterian Church is in the Presbytery of Wyoming. Find this presbytery on the map on page 112.

Word Puzzle

Light the Way

Use the code clues from the Scripture verse to solve the puzzle. You will have to figure out what letters some code signs are.

Code Clues

Y o u   a r e   t h e   l i g h t   o f   t h e   w o r l d .

_ _   _ _ _   _ _ _ _   _ _ _ _ _   _ _ _   _ _ _ _ _ _   _ _ _ _ _

_ _ _ _ _ _   _ _ _ _ _ _ _   _ _   _ _ _ _   _ _ _ _ _   _ _ _ _   _ _ _

_ _ _ _ _   _ _ _ _   _ _ _ _ _ _   _ _ _   _ _ _ _   _ _ _ _ _ _   _ _   _ _ _ _ _

_ _ _ _ _ _ _   _ _   _ _ _ _ _ _ .

(Stuck? Look up Matthew 5:16.)

ord of the Week

Light

Jesus is the light of the world, and he calls us to shine in the world to show God's love.

What You Can Do

Choose a country in this book that especially interests you. Go to the *Mission Yearbook for Prayer & Study* and find the page that tells about the country. Pray for the people whose names are listed there.

Giving What You Have

How many lightbulbs are in your house? Give 2 cents to your church for each one.

PRAYER

O loving God, thank you for the warmth and the sunlight of each day. Help us to be your light, like the churches in the Dominican Republic and the Presbytery of Wyoming. Make us shine for Jesus, in whose name we pray. Amen.

MISSION AROUND THE WORLD

Dominican Republic

Two-thirds of the island of Hispaniola is the Dominican Republic. The other one-third of the island is Haiti. Can you find this island of two countries on the map on page 110? Life is difficult in both countries, but jobs are a little easier to find in the Dominican Republic. As a result, people in Haiti travel across the mountains looking for work. Most Haitians wind up working in the sugar cane fields. They live in ramshackle settlements known locally as *bateys*. In Batey Algodon, Pastor Jack worked with Presbyterian mission co-workers to build a church. After ten years of work by mission teams and Haitians, a chapel was built in Batey Algodon. But the community also needed running water, latrines (toilets), and medical care. After several years of working hard together, Batey Algodon has latrines, and it will soon have water. A clinic is located in a nearby *batey*. The clinic is staffed full-time by a local doctor, and visiting medical groups help with outreach and support. Presbyterian mission

co-workers say, "Not only has the community heard the love of Christ in messages preached in the church, but they have been a part of Christ's love in action."

Batey Algodon volunteers prepare water lines for their community.

MISSION IN THE UNITED STATES
Presbytery of San Juan
Puerto Rico

Living life in Christ means caring for our neighbors. Iglesia Presbiteriana en Caparra Terrace (Caparra Terrace Presbyterian Church) shows Christ's love in action by the care members give to their neighbors. The church, founded in 1954, is in San Juan, Puerto Rico, and part of the Presbytery of San Juan. Can you find this presbytery on the map on page 112? This congregation works to serve and help the children of God in a variety of ways. Three of its programs are Esperanza para la Vejez (Hope for the Elderly), Almacén de Jesús (Jesus' Warehouse), and Centro de Ayuda a la Familia (Family Assistance Center). The Esperanza para la Vejez program helps older adults. Almacén de Jesús provides food, first aid items, and assistance to homeless families and individuals. Centro de Ayuda a la Familia provides counseling services and referrals to mental health professionals. In the Presbytery of San Juan churches work to obey the commandments to "love the Lord your God with all your heart, and with all your soul, and with all your mind" and to "love your neighbor as yourself" (Matthew 22:37, 39).

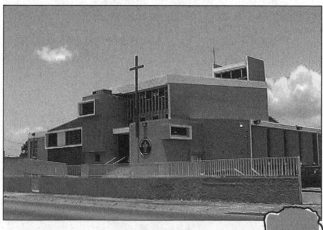

Caparra Terrace Presbyterian Church is in metropolitan San Juan.

SCRIPTURE

Our help is in the name of the LORD, who made heaven and earth (Psalm 124:8).

Craft with Poem

A popular kind of folk art in Latin America is the *retablo*. *Retablos* show scenes from the Bible or tell stories. To make a *retablo* you need a cardboard box (like a shoe box), markers, glue, stiff white paper (like card stock or index cards), and your imagination! Cut one side out of your box. Paint the inside to create a backdrop scene—blue for sky, beige for walls. Paint on clouds or windows. Draw figures on stiff white paper to put into your *retablo*. You may want to draw furniture, animals, trees, or people. Add a tab at the bottom to each figure to help it stand up in your *retablo*. Color and cut out the figures, folding the tab once at the bottom. Arrange your figures to tell the story and glue them down.

Con nuestra fe, somos seguidores.
(With our faith, we are followers.)
Con el amor de Jesús, somos ganadores.
(With Jesus' love, we are winners.)

Word of the Week

Imagine

When you imagine, you can see in your mind the things that might be. Imagine a world where everyone knows that God loves them.

Did You Know?

On July 25, 1898, Puerto Rico became a territory of the United States. Puerto Rican Presbyterians make up the largest group of Hispanic Presbyterians.

What You Can Do

Make a *retablo* of the mission work described on one of these pages. Then use it to give a minute for mission at your church.

PRAYER

God, we can imagine a world where everyone knows you. Help us to make it so. Bless the people in the Presbytery of San Juan and in Jamaica and the Cayman Islands who are making your world better. In the name of your child Jesus we pray. Amen.

MISSION AROUND THE WORLD

Jamaica and the Cayman Islands

Imagine a stately old colonial church building in the heart of tropical Kingston, Jamaica. (Find Jamaica on the map on page 110.) The neighborhood is old and run-down. Many of the people are poor and homeless. Imagine the people who come to the church—people from the city with not much money and people from the suburbs with more money. Imagine them working together in harmony.

Now imagine in the churchyard a primary school and a bakery. Down the lane from the church are some small, beautiful buildings. And still a little further down the lane is an old garage in which exquisite furniture is being made. The school seeks to educate children who might not otherwise go to school. The bakery supplies jobs and bread to the neighborhood. The small, beautiful buildings are housing for people who are homeless. The furniture shop, through the help of the church, gives work and job skills to people who are trying to make a better future. Nobody in the church is rich with money, but all of them are rich in Christ's love and in their giving.

Giving What You Have

How many years since Puerto Rico's 100th anniversary as a territory? (Have you found the year Puerto Rico was formed as a territory on this page yet?) Save 10 cents for each year to put in your coin box for the Pentecost Offering, which most churches will receive on the Day of Pentecost, May 30.

SCRIPTURE

"And remember, I am with you always, to the end of the age" (Matthew 28:20).

How big is El Salvador? What's the population? Find the answers in the Mission Yearbook for Prayer & Study, *page 132, in the gray box.*

MISSION IN THE UNITED STATES

Northwest Presbytery

Puerto Rico

If you put 100 candles on a birthday cake, it would mean a big celebration! One hundred years as a presbytery is a reason to celebrate, too. And there's even more to celebrate—the first woman who's not a member of the clergy has been elected moderator of Northwest Presbytery. Of the 7 students attending the Evangelical Seminary in Rio Piedras, 4 are women—that's something else to celebrate. Another cause for celebration is Presbyterian Women who give "el dólar que construye"—the dollar that helps to build. The group helps women in need in congregations, assists with new mission projects, and develops leadership skills in women so they may better serve their congregations. Celebrate God's work for more than 100 years in Northwest Presbytery!

Find this presbytery on the map on page 112.

Recipe
Salt Dough

You can make lots of amazing things from this recipe. Mix up some and shape into small blocks. Use them to build an El Salvadoran home!

Ingredients

1 cup table salt
2 cups all-purpose flour
1/2 to 1 cup cold water

In a large bowl, mix salt and flour together with a spoon. Gradually add 1/2 cup water and continue to mix. Keep adding water (remaining portion) until you get the desired consistency. Once you can roll it into a ball, knead it on the table for a few minutes. You may need to add another drop or two of water, but don't make it very moist. After you have shaped the dough, let it air dry for about two days. Then sand it and paint it.

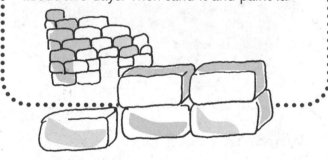

Did You Know?

Since its founding in 1976 by Millard and Linda Fuller, Habitat for Humanity International has built and rehabilitated more than 150,000 houses with families in need.

Giving What You Have

How many places have you lived in? Put 10 cents for each one in your Pentecost Offering coin box.

PRAYER

God, we thank you that the people of El Salvador and Northwest Presbytery in Puerto Rico can rely on you for everything. Help us to rely on you as well. En el nombre de El Salvador, Jesucristo. Amen.

MISSION AROUND THE WORLD

El Salvador

Located on the southwestern coast of Central America, El Salvador is Spanish for "the Savior." Can you find it on the map on page 110? The country suffered from a civil war in the 1980s. Then, just as life was getting back to normal, some destructive natural disasters occurred. The most severe was Hurricane Mitch in 1998. Then earthquakes in 2001 brought more destruction. These disasters left at least 1,200 people dead and more than a million others homeless. Presbyterian Disaster Assistance responded after the earthquakes. It sent mission teams to help with the rebuilding. Those mission teams rebuilt the entire town of La Pinera in Apopa, north of San Salvador. Their work meant that 265 Salvadoran families had new homes.

The mission workers built the new houses out of concrete blocks so they would last for a long time. New houses mean new hope for the people of El Salvador.

W*ord of the Week* Reliance

As Presbyterians, we believe that God is always with us and will help us at all times. We rely on God to guide us as we seek to do God's will.

What You Can Do

Many communities and churches support Habitat for Humanity. Lots of Habitat projects have things that children can do to help in building a house. Find out how you can help build a house with Habitat.

Families like Sandra Alvarenga's live in new homes built by work teams.

MISSION IN THE UNITED STATES

Southwest Presbytery

Puerto Rico

Tercera Iglesia Presbiteriana (Third Presbyterian Church) in the community of Balboa, Mayagüez, in Puerto Rico shares God's love through its older adult ministry. The church cosponsors a center that has been serving older people of the Mayagüez community for the last thirty years. The center offers health services, recreation, outreach, and social activities. Tercera Iglesia Presbiteriana is active there: its members provide breakfast and lunch to participants and medical personnel. Women in Service Ministry is a new program whose members serve as volunteers at the Mayagüez nursing home and help transport patients when they need to go somewhere. But Tercera Presbiteriana doesn't stop at the basic physical and emotional needs of the older adults. It also schedules home visits to share the gospel. Prayer and counseling are all part of the center's community affairs program. The church is in Southwest Presbytery in Puerto Rico. Find Southwest Presbytery on the map on page 112.

Giving What You Have

Do you know many people who are older than 65? Save 5 cents for every older person you know to put in the Pentecost Offering.

SCRIPTURE

There is one body and one Spirit, just as you were called to the one hope of your calling, one Lord, one faith, one baptism (Ephesians 4:4–5).

Craft

Cordel (A Little Book of Poems)

A traditional folk art in Brazil is the *cordel*. This is a book made of inexpensive paper that has a woodcut design on the cover. The books are sold in the marketplace, where the author is often on hand to recite the poems and try to sell the books. Many of them are about Bible stories.

Materials

sponge (3 inches
   wide, 5 inches long,
   1/2 inch thick)
scissors
tempera paint
2 pieces of heavy
   paper (card stock)
several pieces of lightweight paper
paper plate
jute cord
stapler

Cut a simple shape like a cross from the sponge. Pour a little tempera paint out on a paper plate and dip the sponge into the paint. Press the sponge down firmly on one piece of card stock to make the front cover. When the paint is dry, staple the lightweight sheets of paper between the 2 pieces of card stock to make a book. Tie a loop in one end of the cord. Staple the other end to the top left corner of the front book cover. In your *cordel*, write a poem that tells a Bible story, copy a psalm, or make up your own story.

POEMS

MISSION AROUND THE WORLD

Brazil

Many children and teenagers live on the streets in Teixeira de Freitas, a town in Bahia, northeastern Brazil. They have no homes and little direction from loving adults. This was one reason why mission co-workers Michael and Irene Sivalee wanted to start a new church in the town. Brazilians young and old were invited to worship and study the Bible in different people's homes. As the congregation grew, members bought property and built a Presbyterian church. The church members worked to help homeless children and teens with their needs. Irene taught a class of thirty to thirty-five youth four times each week. The youth enjoyed singing and performing drama. One young boy, Marcelo, never missed a program. He was always the first to appear at the church's door. He was eager to learn about God's love and how to share this love with others. That was several years ago, but recently the Sivalees received a letter from Marcelo, saying, "Aunt Irene and Pastor Michael, I was baptized and became a member of the Independent Presbyterian Church in Teixeira de Freitas. I am also serving God as a Sunday school teacher for children. I am very happy."

Find Brazil on the map on page 110.

Marcelo has found joy at the Independent Presbyterian Church in Teixeira de Freitas.

PRAYER

Think about what it means for many different people to be united in Christ. Can you picture how you are a part of the same faith as an older adult in Puerto Rico and of Marcelo in the story about Brazil? Thank God for all our differences and for our unity in Christ. Write a poem prayer about this that you can put in your cordel. Remember that a poem doesn't have to rhyme!

Word of the Week

Unity

Unity means that even though we may be very different, we are all one in Christ.

What You Can Do

Ask how you can help with church school at your church. Here are some ideas: sweep floors after class, help with younger children, serve snacks or water to others, and read Scripture.

Did You Know?

The Presbyterian Constitution, the rules that govern our church, is made up of two books: the *Book of Order* and the *Book of Confessions.*

Pentecost Offering

Word of the Week

Pentecost

Pentecost is from the Greek word for "fiftieth." It's a holy day for both Jews and Christians. The Jews were celebrating it before there were any Christians. They called it the Feast of Weeks, and it came 50 days after Passover. Christians celebrate it 50 days after Easter. That's because of what happened that first Pentecost (Feast of Weeks) after Jesus died and was raised from the dead. He had promised his disciples that the Holy Spirit would come to them to help them after he was gone. And on Pentecost, the Holy Spirit came to the group of disciples in a special way: a noise like a strong wind swept through the room where the disciples were meeting and something like flames of fire rested over their heads. They began to speak in other languages that they didn't even know so that people who spoke those languages could hear about Jesus in their own language. About 3,000 people became followers of Christ that day.

What You Can Do

- Ask your teacher or pastor how your congregation will use its portion of the Pentecost Offering to help children at risk.
- The Day of Pentecost is also called the birthday of the church. Ask your teacher if you can have a birthday party for the church in your church school class.
- Learn more about short-term mission service by reading letters from Young Adult Volunteers like Sarah that are posted on the Web site www.pcusa.org/missionconnections/yav.htm.

SCRIPTURE

"Together with Christ, we will be given what God has promised" (Romans 8:17).

Find the hidden "P" objects in the drawing.

The illustration, by Dennis McKinsey, was drawn from the photograph on the front cover of the Pentecost Offering video.

Parrot	Paintbrush	Pineapple
Pitchfork	Polka Dots	Pie
Peanut	Pig	Pencil
Pliers	Pumpkin	Pyramid
Plane	Pear	Phone

Did You Know?

Children at risk are "at risk" because situations in their lives might keep them from growing up as well as others. Some of the things that can make a child "at risk" are: not enough money to support the family, not having a loving family, or having a serious illness.

MISSION IN THE UNITED STATES

Presbytery of Muskingum Valley

Ohio

Some children go to school without having eaten breakfast and have a hard time doing well in school. In Zanesville, Ohio, Brighton Presbyterian Church does something special for children in their neighborhood with money received from the Pentecost Offering. They provide a hot breakfast and a warm place for children to wait for the bus. Brighton Church calls this program Bus Stop Breakfast. Church members wake up extra early to prepare breakfast and welcome the children. Because of a caring church, children can start off their school day with a healthy breakfast and a hug or smile from someone who cares. Find the Presbytery of Muskingum Valley on the map on page 112.

Brighton Presbyterian Church makes breakfast for neighborhood children.

PRAYER

Dear God, thank you for sending the Holy Spirit to be with us always. Thank you that the Spirit reminds us of ways we can make a difference with our prayers and caring actions. Thank you for your love for us that will never end. In Jesus' name we pray. Amen.

MISSION AROUND THE WORLD

Uruguay

Sarah Henken attended the PC(USA) General Assembly in Fort Worth as a youth delegate in 1999. At the General Assembly she learned about how God works through the Presbyterian Church and its members. Because of that experience Sarah thought a lot about what it would be like to work for the church. In 2002 she joined the PC(USA) Young Adult Volunteer program. Sarah was assigned to Centro del Servicio Social El Pastoreo (center of caring), a ministry of the Waldensian Church in Uruguay. (Find Uruguay on the map on page 110.) Located in Rosario, El Pastoreo is a community center where Sarah taught two- and three-year-olds. This was a great place for her because she loves children and speaks Spanish, the language that is spoken in Uruguay. "As I have come to know the people of El Pastoreo, I am redefining my ideas of living simply, of what things I truly need. I have been richly blessed in so many ways, and I will probably always have more than I truly need," wrote Sarah.

Money from the Pentecost Offering gives young adults like Sarah the chance to learn what it is like to know and share the love of God in a different place.

PENTECOST OFFERING

Did You Know?

The Pentecost Offering is one of four special offerings of the PC(USA). Money that people give to the Pentecost Offering helps children at risk, youth, and young adults. One of the special things about the Pentecost Offering is that congregations get to keep almost half of the offering to help children at risk in their own communities.

Giving What You Have

Surprise your family members some morning this week by preparing breakfast for them. Like the church in Zanesville, you can give someone you care about a special start to his or her day.

Word of the Week

Growing

Just as fruit trees grow and produce fruit, we grow in our faith and produce fruits of the Spirit. You can see those fruits in the mission work of the church, growing in the hearts of those who hear the gospel.

MISSION IN THE UNITED STATES

Nevada Presbytery

Nevada, California

Most people think about casinos, shows, and bright lights when they think about Las Vegas, Nevada. But behind the glittering lights and the flashy attractions are people who suffer from hunger, poverty, and prejudice. Amazing Grace Ministries in Las Vegas serves homeless men, women, and children. The people gather to worship God on Sundays and Wednesdays. Many are reaching out to others who are homeless to offer love. Amazing Grace Ministries also helps people with meals, clothing, furniture, and job and counseling referrals. But most important, they share together the love and grace of God, reaching out in Jesus' name to love one another. This vision for ministry was started by Susan and Gino Maini. Gino likes to say, "It's all about grace!"

Amazing Grace Ministries is in Nevada Presbytery, which you can find on the map on page 112.

SCRIPTURE

By contrast, the fruit of the Spirit is love, joy, peace, patience, kindness, generosity, faithfulness, gentleness, and self-control (Galatians 5:22–23).

Craft

Create the fruits of the spirit. Make beautiful fruits from the salt dough recipe on page 44. Paint them! Make small fruits and use a toothpick to make them into beads. Display them. Wear them. Create your own new fruit and give it a name!

Giving What You Have

Save your extra change or allowance money to buy cans of fruit for your local food bank. Invite your friends to help, and bring these real fruits of your spirit to the food bank.

MISSION AROUND THE WORLD

Peru

Living on the side of one huge hill outside of Lima, Peru, is a group of five women who call themselves Grupo Maná—Patricia, Julia, Emilia, Glendi, and Berta. (Find Peru on the map on page 110.) They participate in the Fair Trade Bridge that links economically disadvantaged artisans of the Joining Hands Against Poverty Network of Peru with the Presbytery of Giddings-Lovejoy. Grupo Maná makes place mats, napkins, table runners, and pastoral stoles from the traditional manta fabric in which Andean women carry their babies. In 2002, through their sewing and participation in the Presbyterian Hunger Program effort, the income of these women grew 350 percent.

"While in their one-room 'workshop' amidst the colorful cloth, the children, and the occasional chickens who wander in and out, I feel surrounded by God's presence," mission co-worker Ruth Farrell writes. These women remind Ruth that being a disciple affects how you do routine tasks. Many Peruvians spend hours getting water, washing clothes, cooking, and doing those things that North Americans do quickly so that they can get to something important or enjoyable. These women look at their daily chores with a different viewpoint—as something they do well each day for their families. They have a strong faith that God knows their hopes and fears and will help them as they endure the difficult and celebrate the unexpected in their lives every day.

Ruth writes, "So why is my soul refreshed each time I climb the hill to see these five women? The witness of their lives refreshes my soul and encourages my own walk with God. I rejoice that God invites us to ascend the hill and stand in God's holy place while we learn the 'dailiness' of discipleship."

Did You Know?

In 2003, the PC(USA) had 322 long-term mission workers serving in 69 countries.

PRAYER

We see the fruits of your Spirit, God, growing everywhere that people speak your word, seek your will, and do your work. We see the fruits of your Spirit in Peru and in Nevada Presbytery. Keep us growing and fruitful to share the good news of your Son, in whose name we pray. Amen.

Grupo Maná—with Ruth Farrell (far right)—display some of the hand-sewn garments they created.

What You Can Do

For the next week focus on one of the fruits of the Spirit and let it live in you. The fruits are love, joy, peace, patience, kindness, generosity, faithfulness, gentleness, and self-control. Then memorize the verse on page 50 and recite it to someone at your church.

"... the fruit of the Spirit is love, joy, peacefulness, kindness, gentleness, and self-control."

SCRIPTURE

"For where two or three are gathered in my name, I am there among them" (Matthew 18:20).

MISSION IN THE UNITED STATES

Presbytery of San Joaquin

California

Do you go to an after-school program? In Ivanhoe, California, the Ivanhoe Youth Center after-school program includes homework and reading help, a computer lab, indoor and outdoor games, cooking and woodworking, and arts and crafts. There is a sewing class, too. In that class the children each make quilts for themselves. Then they make one to give to a child at Valley Children's Hospital. On Wednesday nights the church provides a meal and Bible study. In the summer the youth center is open during the day, Monday through Friday, and has lots more activities. The center prepares a free breakfast and lunch every day for children of the many families who have come from Mexico to work in the United States. Since 1998 the Ivanhoe Youth Center has provided a safe place for children and youth to grow, play, and learn about God's love. Find the Presbytery of San Joaquin on the map on page 112.

Craft
Paper Quilt

Make your own paper quilt like the quilts made at the Ivanhoe Youth Center. The pattern below is called Log Cabin. Cut out a paper square, 6 inches x 6 inches. Then measure and cut 1-inch strips of different colored papers. Arrange the strips on the paper square to match the diagram below, then glue the strips onto the square. The center of the pattern can be the base square. To make a quilt, construct four, six, or eight squares and glue or tape them together. The quilt can be used as a wall hanging. Or make a rectangle and use it as a place mat! If you sew, try making some Log Cabin quilt squares from cloth!

Worship

When we gather for worship, we give honor and love to God, and God is present with us.

MISSION AROUND THE WORLD

Argentina

Have you learned about ratios in school yet? Ratios compare one thing to another: for example, the eastern coast of the United States stretches about 1,000 miles from Maine to Florida. Compare that to Argentina. It is nearly 4,000 miles long, 4 times longer. That's a 4-to-1 ratio. Find Argentina on the map on page 110. This country stretches from the subtropics in the north to include one of the southernmost cities in the world. Argentina is rich in natural resources like lead, zinc, tin, copper, iron ore, petroleum, and uranium.

But there are other ratios that are very sad. There is a crisis in Argentina. Many people do not have jobs. The cost of food keeps going up. Half of the population lives in poverty. Mission co-worker Kathleen Griffin writes, "Our church soup kitchens have been feeding approximately 125 children a week in 2003 compared to about 60 each week last year." That's a 2-to-1 increase.

A Young Adult Volunteer in 2003, Liz Kenyon, served at El Hogar la Casita, a safe place for young boys in transition.

Young boys find a safe place at El Hogar la Casita.

PRAYER

Make a commitment today that you will spend two minutes in prayer every day for the children of the world, including you. It might be hard to remember at first, but once you make it a habit you will find that you easily remember.

Did You Know?

Remember what a YAV is? A YAV is a Young Adult Volunteer. That's a person who spends a year of his or her life to volunteer in mission work. Each year a half dozen young adults and short-term volunteers, as well as global interns (who volunteer for an eight- to twelve-week summer program), come to Argentina and Uruguay.

Giving What You Have

Do you know someone who is hungry? Can you share some food with them? Or maybe that person is hungry for your smile or a note from you. Feed the hungry.

What You Can Do

Hunger is a problem not only in Argentina but in many countries around the world, including the United States. Find out what your church and community are doing about hunger. Talk with your church school teacher about what your class can do.

Word of the Week

Teaching

The Bible tells us that God gives some of us the gift of teaching.

MISSION IN THE UNITED STATES

Presbytery of Boise

Idaho, Nevada

First Presbyterian Church of Boise was founded 126 years ago along the Oregon Trail. On July 15, 1877, the Rev. Sheldon Jackson, a missionary, preached to a group of Presbyterians at the Baptist church. Several months later the First Presbyterian Church was formed with eighteen members—fifteen women and three men.

Ever since, the church has reached out in love to others. At first it was to the people passing by in wagon trains. Now the church provides Friendship Dinners to homeless people in the Boise area. The meals are prepared and served by youth, adults, and friends in other churches. Church members donate the food and eat with the guests at the Friendship Dinner. Third- and fourth-grade children at the church make centerpieces for the tables with the theme "How I See God." Not only do guests get as much as they want to eat, they are also encouraged to take home as much food as they want. The church shows the guests at the banquet the abundance of God's love! Find the Presbytery of Boise on the map on page 112.

SCRIPTURE

Teach me your way, O LORD, that I may walk in your truth; give me an undivided heart to revere your name (Psalm 86:11).

Recipe

Homemade Tortillas

In many countries and in many parts of the U.S. Southwest, tortillas are a part of every meal. And they are easy to make. Ask an adult to help you make this recipe.

Ingredients

3 cups all-purpose flour
1 tsp. salt
1/3 cup vegetable shortening or lard
1 cup warm water

Combine the flour, salt, and shortening in a large bowl and mix together until crumbly. Add water and mix until you can make the dough into a ball. Lightly flour the surface of your counter or table, then place the dough on it and knead for about 5 minutes until the dough is smooth. Cover the dough and let it rest for at least 30 minutes.

Divide the dough into 12 equal portions. Make a ball of each portion by rolling it between the palms of your hands. Again, lightly flour your working surface and use a rolling pin to make each ball into an 8-inch circle. Put sheets of plastic wrap between the circles of dough as you make them. To cook the flour tortillas, heat a heavy skillet over high heat. Place a circle of dough in the pan and cook for 30 seconds. Turn and cook on the other side until it is slightly puffed and speckled brown but is still soft enough to fold, about 30 seconds. Remove and then cook the rest of the tortillas, stacking them as you go. You can eat them immediately or let them cool, wrap them in plastic wrap, and refrigerate for up to 3 days.

MISSION AROUND THE WORLD

Guatemala

A carpenter, a doctor, a construction worker. Men and women, young people and children, a Guatemalan teenager. All were working together. All had heard Jesus' command to love one another. They worked together to build six two-room homes for six single mothers. "I saw Jesus' words come alive under the trees a little way off the dirt road," writes mission co-worker Ellen Dozier. For a week, people from Covenant Presbyterian Church in Madison, Wisconsin, worked with their new friends from Guatemala to build the houses. When the week came to an end everyone gathered in a circle. Songs, tears, laughter, and prayers filled the circle, and the love that Jesus spoke about came alive. Ellen marvels at "what can happen when many different people hear and live out Jesus' commandment to 'love one another.' Homes are built, brothers found, sisters embraced, gifts received, a community begun; a little sign of God's kingdom is now tucked away just off a dirt road under the trees."

Can you find Guatemala on the map on page 110?

The building of homes is a labor of love.

Find out what the Presbytery of Boise has to do with stuffed toys in South Africa. The answer is on the page about the presbytery in the Mission Yearbook for Prayer & Study.

PRAYER

God, bless those who help those who are homeless in Guatemala and in the Presbytery of Boise. Help us to be thankful for all we have, especially the love of your child Jesus. Amen.

What You Can Do

Learn about missions for people who are homeless in your community. Ask your pastor if you can give a minute for mission about people who have no homes and what Presbyterians do to help them.

Did You Know?

The money of Guatemala, a *quetzal*, is named for a beautiful, endangered bird.

Giving What You Have

It takes almost eight *quetzals* to equal one U.S. dollar. What would four *quetzals* equal? Figure out the amount and put it into the church offering plate on Sunday.

General Assembly

Understanding the General Assembly

SCRIPTURE

"I have come in order that you might have life—life in all its fullness" (John 10:10 TEV).

Have you ever thought about how the PC(USA) works? You can see how things work in your own congregation: the session meets and makes a decision, a committee or work group is formed, and then people get to work to make things happen!

In fact, the way we work is so important that our name comes from a very old Greek word for elder: *presbyter*. When your congregation needs to choose leaders, it elects members to the session. Everyone on the session is an elder—a *presbyter*—and all of them are specially called by God to be leaders in the church. The session takes care of the church—looking after the staff, the programs, and the building. Most sessions meet once a month.

It isn't so much different at the presbytery and synod. Take a look at the map on page 112 and see the boundaries for presbyteries and synods. Presbyteries are made up of lots of churches; synods are made up of several presbyteries; and the General Assembly, when it meets, includes people from all of them.

When a presbytery, a geographical group of many congregations, needs to make decisions, the congregations send commissioners to a presbytery meeting. Commissioners are elders who are representatives from their congregations. A representative is someone who speaks and acts for a larger group of people. The people who can vote at a meeting of the presbytery are elder-commissioners and all of the ministers in the presbytery. The elder-commissioners and ministers meet, discuss important plans, and vote on how things will be done. Most presbyteries meet several times a year.

When the whole PC(USA) denomination meets, the meeting is called a General Assembly. Commissioners to a General Assembly are representatives from their presbyteries: ministers and elders. Presbyteries choose and send commissioners to the General Assembly each year to made decisions about how the PC(USA) is going to work.

At the General Assembly, people meet in small groups to study, pray, and talk about the decisions that need to be made. Then they meet in one very large group and vote on the decisions. But that isn't the end of it! Some of the decisions are so important that the people at the General Assembly aren't the only ones who decide. That's when they tell the presbyteries that they need to vote. So the overtures (that's a fancy word for ideas to vote on) are sent to the presbyteries from the General Assembly, and the commissioners at the presbytery meeting vote. Then the votes of all the presbyteries are added up and the decision is made!

If you are thinking some of this sounds familiar (kind of like the way the United States works), you are right! There are town councils and city and county governments, then state legislatures, and then the federal government. Each one has its own special work to do. Different areas of a state send their representatives to the state capital, and each state sends representatives to the national capital.

It is easy to see why it is important to pray for the people and the work of the General Assembly as they meet this week. Ask God to give them wisdom, courage, and strength as they do the hard work of leading our denomination.

Congregations
(write your church name here)

Presbyteries
(write your presbytery name here)

Synods
(write your synod name here)

General Assembly

Words of the Week

Presbyter, Congregation, Presbytery, Synod, General Assembly

PRAYER

Life-giving God, infuse with your Spirit those who gather to do the work of the General Assembly in Richmond, Virginia. We pray that their actions reflect the good news of the gospel for all your children. Bless the work of your church in this place and in every place. In Christ's name. Amen.

photo by David Young

A wonderful parade of banners always brightens the opening session of General Assembly.

Giving What You Have

How many General Assemblies have been held in the Presbyterian Church? Hint: You'll find the number somewhere on this page. Save a penny for each year and put them in the offering plate this Sunday.

What You Can Do

- Pray for the General Assembly this week in Richmond, Virginia. Pray especially for the commissioners from your presbytery.
- Visit your presbytery office and meet the staff. See how many different programs your presbytery has for doing God's work.
- Find out how many congregations are in your presbytery. Ask your friends to help you send a note to the session of each congregation to tell them about the *Children's Mission Yearbook for Prayer & Study*.
- Visit the PC(USA)'s Web site to find out more about the news from this year's General Assembly. The Web address is www.pcusa.org.
- Find out how far you live from the city in which your synod office is located. If it is close enough, travel to the office to see it and meet the staff.

Did You Know?

There are 173 presbyteries and 16 synods in the PC(USA).

Can you find the prayer on this page in the Mission Yearbook for Prayer & Study? (Hint: Look in the Table of Contents under "General Assembly, Call to Prayer" in the Mission Yearbook for Prayer & Study.)

photo by David Young

The Rocky Mountain Children's Choir of Denver sings at Monday evening worship for the 215th General Assembly (2003).

Did You Know?

The General Assembly of the Presbyterian Church (U.S.A.) is meeting this week in Richmond, Virginia. This is the 216th General Assembly!

That all may have life in fullness
John 10:10b

Vocation

Your vocation is your calling, the work in life that God made you to do. What does God call you to do?

SCRIPTURE

We know that all things work together for good for those who love God, who are called according to [God's] purpose (Romans 8:28).

MISSION IN THE UNITED STATES

Presbytery of Cayuga-Syracuse

New York

The people of the congregations in the Presbytery of Cayuga-Syracuse have some things in common with churches in Pyongyang Presbytery, South Korea. People love Jesus Christ, pray, sing, and worship God in similar ways. The Presbyterians on both sides of the world attend school, work in businesses, love their children, enjoy eating at family gatherings, celebrate holidays, offer generous hospitality to friends and strangers, and support mission projects that help other people at home and around the world. Even the four seasons are similar. During the last four years, the groups have participated in many exchange trips. It started with adults visiting each others' country for twelve days. Then older youth in high school and college visited, traveled, and attended the Presbyterian Youth Triennium together. Later, Korean children ages nine through fifteen lived in central New York with host families for a month in order to improve their English language skills. These visits to churches and homes have allowed many friendships to form. Through the presbytery partnership, church members who would never have known each other now pray for each other. Find the Presbytery of Cayuga-Syracuse on the map on page 112.

Craft

Long ago in Korea, people made up dances that included dialogue, like little skits, to poke fun at unpopular rulers and high society. But the dancers used masks so they wouldn't be recognized. The Korean masked dance is now a popular folk dance.

The masks have a black cloth in the back. Red, white, and black colors are used. The older person's mask is black, a young man's is red, and a young woman's is white. Most masks are of human faces, but some are of animals.

To make a mask, use a paper plate. Draw a face on the plate. Cut out eye holes. You may want to have someone help you measure them, so you'll be able to see out.

Paint your mask in the color of the character you want. Make several and put on a play!

Did You Know?

We celebrate Independence Day this week. So many Presbyterians fought for American independence that sometimes people call the American Revolution "the Presbyterian Rebellion." When the 1787 and 1788 synods met, the Presbyterian Church took a stand against slavery and recommended that Presbyterians work to end slavery In America.

Giving What You Have

The Declaration of Independence was signed in 1776. The Constitution of the United States didn't take effect until 1789. How many years passed between the signing of the Declaration and the Constitution taking effect? For each year, put 5 cents into the church offering plate on Sunday.

What You Can Do

Read a book about people with disabilities. Check your school or public library for sources. Some possibilities are:

What It's Like to Be Me, edited by Helen Exley, Friendship Press

Andy Finds a Turtle, by Nan Holcomb, Jason and Nordic Publishers

Ask your school librarian for other suggestions.

PRAYER

God, we thank you for the many ways in which you make things work together for good for your people. We ask that you continue to bless the people of Korea, the work at Hanil Seminary, and the partnership of the Presbytery of Cayuga-Syracuse with Pyongyang Presbytery. Help us to be always aware of your work in our world. In Jesus' name. Amen.

MISSION AROUND THE WORLD

South Korea

Have you ever thought about what life would be like if you had a disability? Or maybe you have a disability or know someone who does. If so, you know that a few simple changes can help a person with a disability in many ways. Daniel and Carol Chou Adams are professors at Hanil University and Presbyterian Theological Seminary in Jeonju, South Korea. When Hanil University moved to its new campus, changes were made to improve the lives of persons with disabilities. All campus buildings were built with ramps for wheelchairs so that all people would be able to enjoy the same access to buildings. Wheelchairs and electric carts are now a common sight on the campus. In chapel services, interpreters translate words into sign language. This inclusiveness among the faculty, staff, and student body has become contagious. Today, Hanil University and Presbyterian Theological Seminary is a leader in providing access to all of God's people in all of its programs.

Find South Korea on the map on page 110.

Hanil University students lead a summer program for children.

Rehabilitation Through the Arts is a respected theater program that sends a positive message to the prison population.

MISSION IN THE UNITED STATES

Presbytery of Hudson River

New York

Presbyterians in the Presbytery of Hudson River go to prison! Yes, it is true! That's because recently the presbytery became partners with Rehabilitation Through the Arts, a theater program that brings live theater to Sing Sing Prison in Ossining, New York. In the fall of 2002, ninety members from the presbytery were invited inside the prison to the performance of a hilarious play called *Stratford's Decision*. The inmates of the prison wrote and acted in the play. *Stratford's Decision*, which caught the attention of the *New York Times*, is set in the time of Shakespeare and Queen Elizabeth I of England (late 1500s). The actors mostly used language appropriate for that time, but they would also use contemporary street talk that sounded funny when mixed with the language of Shakespeare. The theater program helps prisoners by getting them involved in creative activities. It helps them feel better about themselves. And it helps the people on the outside know more about how people in prison are real people.

Find the Presbytery of Hudson River on the map on page 112.

SCRIPTURE

"Then he will answer them, 'Truly I tell you, just as you did not do it to one of the least of these, you did not do it to me' " (Matthew 25:45).

Recipe
Rice

In Japan, as in many countries, rice is an important food. To make great rice, first get permission to cook. Then, put 2 cups water into a heavy saucepan that has a lid. Bring the water to a boil over medium heat. When it is boiling add 1 cup rice. Stir the rice in, turn the heat down as low as it will go, and put the lid on the pan. Let it cook for about 20 minutes,* until all the water is absorbed. Eat and enjoy!

*Check the package the rice came in for the length of time to cook. Some kinds of rice take longer than 20 minutes.

MISSION AROUND THE WORLD

Japan

What is your favorite subject in school? Mission co-worker Carol Hastings's favorite time of the week is English class! Six Japanese women and one Korean woman come to practice their English in a class Carol leads in Tokyo, Japan. (Find Japan on the map on page 110.) They discuss all kinds of topics. One day in a discussion of family reunions, the South Korean woman, Mrs. Soh, shared the story of her family. Just before she was born, Mrs. Soh's father escaped from North Korea. He left his five-year-old daughter and one-year-old son with relatives. The government of North Korea would not allow him to return. For fifty-one years he could not hear any news of his family, and he could not send any news to them. Early in 2003, Mrs. Soh's elderly father was finally granted permission to return to North Korea for a short visit with his daughter. Even though Mrs. Soh's father was very sad when he returned home, Mrs. Soh was glad he had been able to see his family again. The English class learned more than English the day she told her father's story.

What You Can Do

Send greetings from your church school or family to the Hastings family in Japan. You can find the address on the PC(USA) Web site www.pcusa.org/missionconnections.

PRAYER

There are so many different kinds of people in the world, God, and you love every one of them. Help those who do your work in Japan and in the Presbytery of Hudson River. Let those who are in prison know that you care for them. In Jesus' name. Amen.

Word of the Week

Transformation

Haiku is a form of poetry from Japan. It has five syllables in the first line, seven in the second, and five in the third. Here is an example:

God's love changes us

Like the warm sun melts the ice

A transformation!

Did You Know?

The game we call Rock Paper Scissors in the United States is called Jan Ken Po in Japan.

Giving What You Have

Count the number of children in your church school class. If there are more than 10, contribute 25 cents to your church on Sunday. If there are fewer than 10, contribute 10 cents to your church.

MISSION IN THE UNITED STATES

Presbytery of Elizabeth

New Jersey

Do you know what *agape* means? It is a Greek word for "love"—not the mushy, romantic kind of love, but the kind of love Jesus has for all of us. So Agape Community Kitchen is a name that says a lot. A group of young people from the Presbyterian Church of Westfield started a soup kitchen in First Presbyterian Church, Elizabeth, New Jersey. Agape Community Kitchen welcomes anyone who is hungry to a hot meal every Wednesday night between 5:00 and 6:00 all year long. Usually between 175 and 240 guests are there for supper. Three Presbyterian churches work

SCRIPTURE

Owe no one anything, except to love one another; for the one who loves another has fulfilled the law (Romans 13:8).

at Agape on a regular basis, and volunteers from several other churches in the presbytery help. Agape also involves people of all ages, but perhaps not in the typical way. Adult volunteers who come to help will most likely get their work directions from a young person. After the meal, adults and youth share what they learned and saw during the meal. Agape Community Kitchen continues to teach the important lesson of what it means to minister to others.

Agape Community Kitchen is in Elizabeth Presbytery, which you can find on the map on page 112.

Word Puzzle: Alphabet Soup

Agape Presbyterian Church is having a potluck supper. Everyone is supposed to bring a different kind of food. Six families are serving soup. The families are to serve their soup in alphabetical order—of their names, not of the soup names! They all brought different kinds of soup, but the bowls are identical! Help the kitchen workers by figuring out which family brought which soup and where each soup should be placed in the serving line. Mark a dot ● when you know which family brought a soup; mark an ✖ to show the family did NOT bring a soup. The Salisbury family soup is marked to get you started.

Clues:
1. The miso is at one end of the line.
2. The tomato soup will be served immediately before the borscht.
3. The Chen family's soup will be served immediately after the tomato soup and right before the chicken noodle soup.

	Clam Chowder	Chicken Noodle	Tomato	Miso	Borscht	Split Pea
Alberto						✖
Baker						✖
Chen						✖
Ivanoff						✖
Romero						✖
Salisbury	✖	✖	✖	✖	✖	●

Answers and Explanation of Clues:

Alberto – miso
Baker – tomato
Chen – borscht
Ivanoff – chicken noodle
Romero – clam chowder
Salisbury – split pea

1. Since the miso is at one end of the line and we've been told the Salisburys brought the split pea soup, the Alberto family brought the miso.

2. The borscht can't be the Bakers, since the tomato soup will come before it. The tomato soup can't be the Romeros, since the borscht will come after it. The Chens aren't serving either the tomato or chicken noodle

3. The Chens aren't serving either the tomato or chicken noodle soup, but between them. Since the borscht is served after the tomato soup, the borscht belongs to the Chens and the tomato soup belongs to the Bakers. That means the Ivanoffs serve the chicken noodle soup.

4. All that's left is the clam chowder, so that must be the Romeros' soup.

Word of the Week

Covenant

A covenant is a solemn agreement. God makes covenants with us, and God keeps covenants.

MISSION AROUND THE WORLD

New Zealand

The Maori are the people who first settled in New Zealand. Their word for the land of New Zealand is Aotearoa, which means "land of the long white cloud." Find New Zealand on the map on page 110. The Presbyterian Church of Aotearoa New Zealand is the country's third largest denomination with over 400,000 people registering as Presbyterian in the last census. It was founded 160 years ago by Scottish settlers, but now it is becoming a "Kiwi" church, which means it is more a church of New Zealand and not of Scotland. The church has a Maori synod, a Pacific Island synod with representatives from all the island groups within the church, and a growing Asian membership. Even the inclusion of the word *Aotearoa* in the name of the denomination shows a strong commitment to include native peoples who lived in New Zealand before European immigrants arrived.

Did You Know?

The Maori people are famous for their singing. They have many types of songs: *waiata* songs are sad songs. *Waiata tangi* are songs of weeping and are sung when someone has died. *Waiata ahore* are love songs, and *waiata whaiaapo* are songs for a beloved one.

PRAYER

God, you have kept your promises through the work of your churches in New Zealand and in the Presbytery of Elizabeth. Help us to keep our promises to you, through the grace of our Lord, Jesus. Amen.

What You Can Do

Next time you are in worship, find the Psalms in your hymnal. Look at the many ways we can sing to God. Choose a song to sing to God, giving thanks for God's covenants.

photo by the Rev. Tina McCormick

Youth from the Presbytery of Elizabeth also help out in their church's clothes closet.

Giving What You Have

How many songs do you know? See if you can list them all. For every song you can think of put 5 cents into the offering plate on Sunday.

MISSION IN THE UNITED STATES

Presbytery of Shenandoah

Virginia, West Virginia

The Rev. Lyle Moffett must have dreamed of doing mission work. He gave a generous gift that is helping the Presbytery of Shenandoah do God's work. (Find the Presbytery of Shenandoah on the map on page 112.) Money from the Lyle Moffett Grant Fund supports work in the Rapps Mill community, which is in an isolated area of Rockbridge County. The region has many elderly adults who live in poverty and young people with low-paying jobs and little education. But Rapps Mill Community Church is a bright light shining in this community. Oxford Presbyterian Church supports the Rapps Mill church by providing a pastor. Moffett's gift funds an after-school program that provides educational, nutritional, and spiritual nourishment to the children and adults of the community. Job training, homework help, and new friends in the community encourage hope for the happiness of future generations. The Lyle Moffett Grant Fund has helped to make Lyle Moffett's dream a reality.

Word of the Week

Stewardship

In Bible times, the steward made certain everything in the household was taken care of for the owner. Stewardship is how we do this and means taking good care of the gifts God has given us.

SCRIPTURE

When they saw him, they worshiped him; but some doubted (Matthew 28:17).

Craft
Pandanus Leafmark

You probably don't have any pandanus trees in your backyard, but you can weave with paper just like Emily and Kinsey in Vanuatu weave with pandanus leaves.

Cut a leaf shape about 6 inches long and 3 inches wide. Fold the leaf in half the long way and make four or five cuts about 1 1/2 inches long.

Cut four strips of paper (they can be any color) 1/2 inch wide and 3 inches long.

Weave them alternately back and forth through the cut strips on the leaf.

Sign and date your leafmark and use it to mark your place when you take a break from reading.

Giving What You Have

How many books are in the Bible? Give 1 cent in the offering plate on Sunday for each book of the Bible. If you have read any of the books in the Bible, add 1 cent more!

Leann teaches Kinsey about a pandanus leaf.

What You Can Do

Make some Bible bookmarks and give them to your friends at church. Write this verse on the back: If any of you is lacking in wisdom, ask God, who gives to all generously and ungrudgingly, and it will be given you (James 1:5).

If any of you is lacking in wisdom, ask God who gives to all generously and ungrudgingly and it will be given you. *James 1:5*

PRAYER

God, your work in Vanuatu and in the Presbytery of Shenandoah shows your great love for all people. Help us to be good stewards of all your gifts, sharing your love with all people everywhere, doing all we do in the name of Jesus. Amen.

MISSION AROUND THE WORLD
Vanuatu

Emily, age thirteen, sits under a pandanus tree. She's a long way from Montana, where she used to live. Emily takes classes at Onesua Presbyterian High School in Vanuatu. (Find Vanuatu on the map on page 110.) Her parents, Bruce and Lora Whearty, are teachers there. Onesua is a boarding school for about 400 boys and girls in grades seven through twelve. Students study traditional subjects such as English, French, math, and science, as well as religious education. Bruce teaches English and mathematics. Lora teaches a kindergarten class for the children of the school's staff with Leann, the woman on the left in the picture. Emily and her sister Kinsey both take classes at Onesua, but they also are learning outside school. In the photo, Leann is teaching Kinsey how to strip the central rib from a pandanus leaf so that it is ready to dry for weaving projects. Leann's husband, Mark, the man on the ladder, helped pull down the leaves from the tree in the background. He was surprised to learn that pandanus trees do not grow in Montana. Lora says, "Mission is not something 'we' do to or for 'them'; it's the adventure of learning from each other!"

Did You Know

You can read more stories about mission in the United States and more of the Wheartys' letters, including letters from the girls, at the PC(USA) mission Web site, www.pcusa.org/missionconnections.

Word of the Week

Power

Just like electric power makes lights come on, God's power makes the light of love shine!

MISSION IN THE UNITED STATES

National Capital Presbytery

Metropolitan Washington, D.C.

Glenkirk is the outdoor ministry of National Capital Presbytery, and it is located in Gainesville, Virginia. Find National Capitol Presbytery on the map on page 112. Every year about six hundred campers come to this summer camp. They experience living in a community where they can get to know and trust one another. Campers live in a "village group" that serves as their family for the week. During their time at camp, the village members do all their activities together, including eating meals family-style around a big table in the woods. The campers work together to cook one meal each day in the village. One of the main reasons for the village group is to help children know a true sense of community. Children and youth need to feel accepted and loved, wherever they are in their faith journey and life journey. At Glenkirk campers hear about and experience God's love for everyone.

photo by Paul Jeffrey/ACT

Glenkirk campers prepare for high adventure rock climbing.

SCRIPTURE

The light shines in the darkness, and the darkness did not overcome it (John 1:5).

Recipe

Xingren Dangang
(shing-RUN DAHN-gahng)
(Almond Cookies)

Makes 7 to 8 dozen

Ingredients

1 cup shortening or margarine
3/4 cup sugar
2 eggs
1 tbs. almond extract
2 1/2 to 3 cups flour
1/2 tsp. baking soda
1/4 tsp. salt
1 egg white
almond halves (optional)

Cream together shortening or margarine and sugar in large bowl. Add eggs one at a time and almond extract. In another bowl combine flour, baking soda, and salt.

Using your fingers, mix dry ingredients with wet mixture into a fairly stiff dough. Divide dough in half. On a floured surface, roll each half with your hands into a log 1 foot long and 1 1/2 inches in diameter. Wrap dough in waxed paper and refrigerate 3 hours. When it is chilled and you are ready to bake, preheat oven to 375°F.

Beat 1 egg white lightly with a whisk. Cut cookies into 1/4-inch slices and place on ungreased cookie sheets. If you like, you can press an almond half in the center of each cookie. Brush with egg white and bake 10 minutes. After removing them from the oven let the cookies cool off on a rack on the counter. Eat and enjoy!

Giving What You Have

How many of the almond cookies that you made did you eat? For each cookie, give 5 minutes of time helping someone in your family. This too, shows the power of God's love.

MISSION AROUND THE WORLD

Taiwan

One evening mission co-worker John McCall spoke to a youth group in a church in Taiwan's Taipei County. Find Taiwan on the map on page 110. Before the talk, the youth led a time of singing. John noticed a young man who sang enthusiastically. This young man asked John several questions after the talk. John learned the young man had been a Christian only about a year and was eager to tell the story about how he came to know Christ. Pointing to another young man who had been playing the drums during the singing, the young Christian shared, "He is a high school classmate who asked me to come to his church. I started going with him and the youth group began to feel like a family. They introduced to me their best friend, Jesus Christ, who also has become my best friend." Now this young man rides a bus for over an hour to come to the church each week. He is enthusiastic about his new faith, and perhaps he will invite another classmate to meet his best friend.

The boy playing the drums invited his high school classmate to church.

PRAYER

God of all people, thank you for Jesus, who shows us what it means to be a truly loving friend. Help me to be a friend to those around me by reaching out in some way to someone new. I pray for people in Taiwan and in National Capital Presbytery. In Jesus' name. Amen.

Did You Know?

Many people who go to church for the first time decided to go because a friend invited them!

How many mission workers now serving overseas were appointed to service before you were born? You can figure out the answer by looking in Appendix B, pages 370–374, in the Mission Yearbook for Prayer & Study. *Hint: The year a person was appointed is in parentheses after that person's name.*

What You Can Do

Be a light shining in the darkness! Invite a friend to come to church with you. Let your friend know what your faith means to you.

MISSION IN THE UNITED STATES

Presbytery of Coastal Carolina

North Carolina

Where do you go to church if you mostly live on board a ship? Each year about 300 ships from all over the world dock at the port of Wilmington, North Carolina. In 1972, the Presbytery of Coastal Carolina started the International Seamen's Service. Each year crew members from more than fifty nations receive Christian hospitality at the Seaman's Center. Visitors to the center may worship in the chapel and are offered Bibles. Seafarers can call or e-mail family and friends back home. They can use exercise equipment, watch TV and videos, and read books. Chaplains visit each ship to offer counseling and hold religious services on

board. Chaplains and volunteers provide transportation when crew members need to visit doctors and dentists or pick up supplies. Even far from home, seafarers can find a place where Presbyterians share God's love.

Find the Presbytery of Coastal Carolina on the map on page 112.

Seafarers visit the Seaman's Center in Wilmington.

SCRIPTURE

You open your hand, satisfying the desire of every living thing (Psalm 145:16).

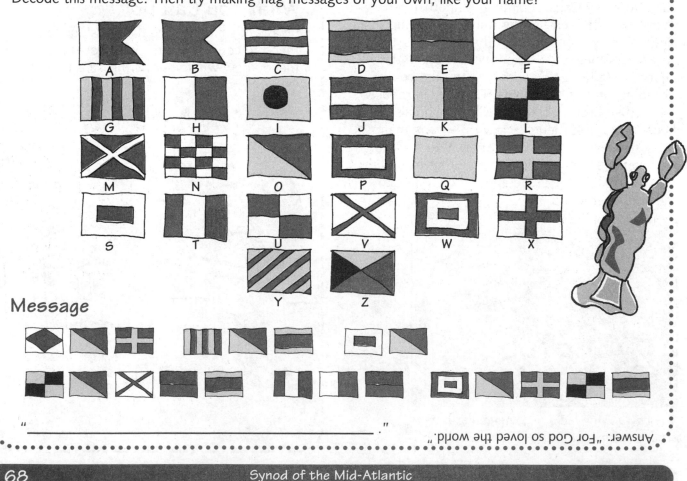

Word Puzzle: Maritime Message

This is the International Maritime Flag alphabet, used by seafarers to communicate at sea. Decode this message. Then try making flag messages of your own, like your name!

Message

Answer: "For God so loved the world."

MISSION AROUND THE WORLD

Philippines

Mary Nebelsick, mission co-worker in the Philippines, tells us about one of her students: "In one of my classes I asked my students to write on courage. One student, Joel, wrote, 'Courage is the strength, directness, and determination of the soul in the face of danger.' Life in the rural Philippines is difficult for most families, and Joel's family was no exception. Their small farm could not support them. Both of his parents also worked for neighbors just to make ends meet. The old house where they lived leaked, and it shook whenever anyone walked in it. During the typhoons Joel and his family ran to the church for safety. There they found a refuge for life. Joel's father became a lay leader and Sunday school teacher. He found time to bring Joel to services and church meetings. Joel committed his life to the parish ministry at the age of twelve. But his father's death soon afterward threatened to end Joel's dream of becoming a pastor. 'Despite these tragic events,' Joel writes, 'we had my mother's strong dedication, and faith in God has sustained us to remain firm and hopeful on God. My mother is so convinced that God will always sustain us and never forsake us.' Bit by bit, the family members fought for their dreams. Kindhearted strangers pledged support for Joel's studies. At sixteen Joel was the youngest student in the seminary class. He was asked to pastor a small rural church when he was only seventeen. This church had never before had its own pastor. The church was dying—it had no budget, no program of activities. Hardly anyone came to services, but God helped Joel to minister and work with the people of the church. 'In a few years we witnessed a revival in the parishioners' Christian life and commitment,' says Joel. 'Indeed, by the courage God gave me and to the church in Santa Cruz we witnessed how God works in marvelous, surprising, and unexpected ways.'"

Find the Philippines on the map on page 110.

PRAYER

God, your generosity is what helps the Presbytery of Coastal Carolina reach out to those at sea. Your strength and courage are what help Joel be a pastor in the Philippines. Help me to be courageous when I feel afraid, knowing that you are generous in giving me your strength. In Jesus' name. Amen.

Giving What You Have

Joel pastored a church when he was seventeen. How old is your pastor? Put 1 cent for each year of your pastor's age into your church's offering plate this week.

Word of the Week

Generosity

God's generosity means that God never stops loving us, never stops caring for us, never gives up on us.

What You Can Do

Look for symbols and signs of God's generosity this week. Make a list of all the ways God is generous to you.

shelter teachers friends

Did You Know?

There are many stories of boats on lakes and seas in the New Testament. Look in the Gospel of Luke to find one of them. (See, for instance, Luke 8:22–25.)

SCRIPTURE

"I am the bread of life. Whoever comes to me will never be hungry, and whoever believes in me will never be thirsty" (John 6:35).

MISSION IN THE UNITED STATES

Presbytery of Southern Kansas

Hoping to follow Jesus' directive in the Scripture passage from John 21:17, "Feed my sheep," the Presbytery of Southern Kansas is working with others in town to find a way to reach out to the neighborhood. That is how Friendship Feast got started. First Presbyterian Church in Dodge City, Kansas, hosts Friendship Feast. This ministry provided nearly 30,000 meals in two years. People in the community volunteer to fix and serve the meals. Each weekday they serve up fellowship and food to people. The only requirement is to be hungry! Sharing a hot meal is a wonderful way to make new friends and learn about the love of God. Because they want to follow Jesus, the churches of the Presbytery of Southern Kansas seek to love and feed the people of their communities by operating food banks, delivering food baskets, and providing hot meals for older adults and anyone who is hungry. Find the Presbytery of Southern Kansas on the map on page 112.

Each weekday Friendship Feast serves a hot lunch to people who are hungry.

Craft
Calligraphy

Here are some words written in Chinese calligraphy. Try your hand at calligraphy by painting some of these Chinese characters. You will need a small paintbrush, black paint, a little water for your brush, and good quality, heavy paper.

日 Sun

月 Moon

山 Mountain

雨 Rain

木 Tree

photo by Joan Erickson

Giving What You Have

What does a loaf of bread cost at your grocery store? Put that amount into the offering plate on Sunday.

What You Can Do

Often, summer is a difficult time for food pantries and food banks that help people with groceries. Help organize a summer food drive for your local food bank.

PRAYER

Jesus, Bread of Life, continue to feed those who are hungry through the loving hands of the people in the Presbytery of Southern Kansas. Let the people of China know your love through the love of your mission workers. Bless us all as we seek to follow you. In Jesus' name. Amen.

MISSION AROUND THE WORLD
China

Mission co-workers Susan and Jay Boone are moving to the city of Wuhan in the eastern part of China. It is on the Yangtze River. Wuhan is a large city, with about 6.5 million people. They will be teaching at one of the national teacher's universities. Susan and Jay enjoy teaching people who may become teachers. Susan will be teaching a group from the university in a program that will help teachers to learn how to teach their courses in English. The Chinese Ministry of Education plans to have 20 percent of all university courses taught in English within the next five years! Jay will be teaching for the Economics Department. Both Susan and Jay will teach Chinese teachers in English, so that their students (who are also teachers) will learn English AND the subject being taught!

Find China on the map on page 110.

W ord of the Week Devotion

信

Devotion means one is very dedicated or loyal to a person or a cause. It also can be an act of prayer or private worship. We are devoted to follow Jesus.

Did You Know?

Kansas has been called the "bread basket of the world" because so much wheat is grown there.

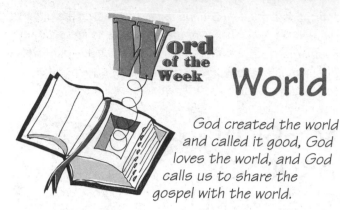

Word **of the Week**

World

God created the world and called it good, God loves the world, and God calls us to share the gospel with the world.

MISSION IN THE UNITED STATES

Presbytery of Giddings-Lovejoy

Missouri, Illinois

Do you remember hearing about the troubles in Bosnia and Herzegovina? Many people left there and came to live in the United States. A few years ago, St. Louis became the new home for a great number of families from Bosnia. Often, immigrants settle in a neighborhood together so that they are able to give each other support. And that is what happened near Southampton Presbyterian Church in St. Louis. Church members wanted to reach out with Christ's love to their new neighbors. They organized a day school for the Bosnian children that now serves between eight and twenty-five children each day. A church staff member manages the school and visits families in their homes to help them with language and immigration problems. Volunteers from Southampton, First Presbyterian Church of Kirkwood, and Kirkwood Baptist Church assist children with their homework during school hours. Children also participate in fun activities like ice skating. The Bosnian families can see Christ's light in the actions of their neighbors at the church.

Southhampton Presbyterian Church is in the Presbytery of Giddings-Lovejoy. Find this presbytery on the map on page 112.

SCRIPTURE

"I am the light of the world. Whoever follows me will never walk in darkness but will have the light of life" (John 8:12).

Recipe
After-School Snack Mix

Ingredients
- 4 cups unsweetened breakfast cereal like Chex, Cheerios
- 1 cup small pretzels
- 1 cup popped popcorn
- 1 cup peanuts or other nuts if you want
- 3 tbs. butter or margarine, melted
- 1 tbs. Worcestershire sauce
- 1 tsp. seasoned salt

Mix cereal, pretzels, and popcorn together in large bowl. If you want nuts, add them also. In a separate bowl, mix together the butter or margarine, Worcestershire sauce, and salt. Drizzle this over the cereal mix. Bake in oven at 350°F for 10 minutes until dry and crisp. Stir. Let cool. Enjoy. If you have any left over, store in a resealable plastic bag or tightly closed container so it will stay fresh. Don't forget to turn your oven off!

MISSION AROUND THE WORLD

Fiji

One great part of having friends is they help when you need them. Sometimes friends help even though they are far away. The Fiji Islands are in the South Pacific, almost 2,000 miles east of Australia. In January 2003, Cyclone Aml struck the Fiji Islands. The cyclone had winds of more than 130 miles per hour with very heavy rains. Crops, homes, and businesses were destroyed. The government of Fiji estimated the damage at about $30 million. Things looked pretty bad, but a friend stepped in. A church that the PC(USA) works closely with, the Uniting Church in Australia, immediately sent a gift of money to help the people in Fiji. The money was used to help those

who had lost homes because of the storm. People in Fiji received the help they needed and learned that a church friend almost 2,000 miles away cared about them. God's people are good friends to those in need even when they are far away.

Find the Fiji Islands on the map on page 110.

Strong winds that blow trees cause major damage in Fiji.

PRAYER

Light of the world, may your love brighten my life as it has the lives of Bosnian children in the Presbytery of Giddings-Lovejoy. We pray for their continued care as they adjust to their new home. We also pray for children who have suffered from severe weather in Fiji. Thank you for your love for the world. In Jesus' name. Amen.

Did You Know?

The Labor Day holiday is coming up. This is not just a day you don't go to school, but a day to honor everyone who works. The first Labor Day holiday was celebrated on Tuesday, September 5, 1882, in New York City.

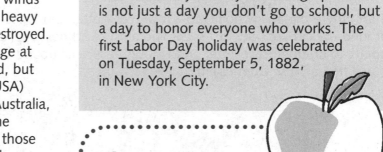

Giving What You Have

How many teachers have you had so far in school? Give 5 cents to your church on Sunday for every teacher you have had.

What You Can Do

Ask for permission to make several batches of the recipe on the opposite page. Put the snack mix into small bags and take them as a treat to an after-school program or to your church school.

SCRIPTURE

I will give thanks to the LORD with my whole heart; I will tell of all your wonderful deeds (Psalm 9:1).

What You Can Do

This is the time of year when most kids are getting back to school after a summer break. Pray for your teachers and school workers that God will give them plenty of wisdom and strength and a good sense of humor!

Word Puzzle: Learning Curve

Start where the arrow points to a lowercase letter and follow the lowercase letters around the circle clockwise. You'll find a list of school supplies. Start where the arrow points to an uppercase letter and follow the letters around the circle counterclockwise. You'll find a verse from Psalm 9.

MISSION AROUND THE WORLD

Ethiopia

Jo Ann Griffith came to teach at Bethel Evangelical Secondary School in 1970. Bethel Evangelical is in the western regional capital of Dembi Dollo, a twelve-hour, bumpy car ride from the capital of Ethiopia, Addis Ababa. It is one of two schools operated in Dembi Dollo by the Ethiopian Evangelical Church Mekane Yesus (EECMY). Mekane Yesus means "dwelling place of Jesus" in Geez, Ethiopia's ancient church language. Jo Ann lives in a dormitory with thirty-six girls and enjoys the deep relationships that have grown between her and the Ethiopian students and staff. Jo Ann writes, "I serve not only as dorm mother but I also seek to be their friend and sister in Christ."

Find Ethiopia on the map on page 110.

Jo Ann Griffith has served in Ethiopia with the Presbyterian Church for forty-five years.

Did You Know?

The PC(USA) has over 100 mission co-workers in Africa. Presbyterian mission workers from the United States have been going to Ethiopia since 1919.

PRAYER

Dear God, in Ethiopia and in Heartland Presbytery children love to learn. Help us to pay attention so we can be good learners and students. And help us to teach everyone about your love through your son Jesus. Amen.

MISSION IN THE UNITED STATES

Heartland Presbytery

Kansas, Missouri

Southridge Presbyterian Church members had just finished setting up a booth at the Heartland Presbytery Mission Fair. A woman and her elementary school-age daughter approached a table displaying school supplies. The church members told the woman that they collected school supplies each August and gave them to the school across the street for students who did not have the supplies they needed. They explained that the supplies were on the table to demonstrate the church's important mission with the school. The woman told the church members that her daughter needed school supplies and asked if she could please have those supplies on the table for her daughter. The church members looked at each other and then gave the woman and her daughter all the school supplies on the table. The mission fair became mission in action.

Find Heartland Presbytery on the map on page 112.

Giving What You Have

Look at all your school supplies. Are there a few you can spare? Take them to your teacher and offer them for kids in your school who may need some extra supplies this time of year.

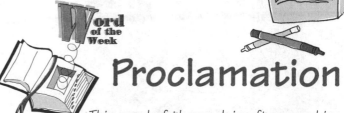

Proclamation

This word of the week is often used in our worship bulletins. When we proclaim the word of God, we are telling people of God's goodness.

MISSION IN THE UNITED STATES

Holston Presbytery

Tennessee

Do you all speak Spanish? That's a question you might ask in Holston Presbytery. Find this presbytery on the map on page 112. In other parts of the United States, the Hispanic population is growing. In upper east Tennessee the Spanish-speaking population has more than doubled! The Holston Presbytery Mission Committee, working with other groups in the community, is providing lots of services for Hispanics. One exciting project teaches English-speaking people to speak Spanish. A group of forty to sixty presbytery members are studying Spanish with the help of their new neighbors from Mexico. Through sharing music, food, stories, and language, they are building new friendships. They can share a deeper understanding of common needs and interests. Some plans include sharing recreational activities with farm workers, attending Spanish-language events and worship services together, and helping all to have equal access to education and health care.

SCRIPTURE

I declare that your steadfast love is established forever; your faithfulness is as firm as the heavens (Psalm 89:2).

Craft

Prayer Beads

People of faith throughout history have used beads to help them focus their prayers. Try to make these simple prayer beads.

Materials

1 one-inch key-chain ring
beads (Use colors and sizes that you like. Pony beads work well. Be sure the beads will fit on the cord.)
cord (about 10 inches long)

Double the cord over and put the looped end through the ring. Thread the two loose ends through the loop and pull the cord tight to keep it on the ring. On one side of the cord, string beads that will remind you of you and your family—brothers, sisters, parents, grandparents, or pets. Be sure to leave enough cord to tie. Make a knot in the end of the cord. On the other side of the cord, string beads that will remind you of your faith—blue for baptism, red for Pentecost, green for growth. Knot the end or tie the two ends together. Use your beads when you pray.

Giving What You Have

How many different kinds of vegetables are in your house or in your garden? Count canned, frozen, and fresh ones. Put 5 cents in the offering plate on Sunday for each variety.

PRAYER

Use your prayer beads to help you focus on praying for others. As you touch a bead, pray for someone in your family. With the remaining beads, think of things you are thankful for and thank God for them.

Did You Know?

Malawi is known as the "warm heart of Africa."

MISSION AROUND THE WORLD

Malawi

Are you ready to do some math? You live in Malawi. (Find Malawi on the map on page 110.) You have eight children. You earn $18 each month. One bag of corn costs $10 plus $2 tax. You also have to pay other bills. How do you survive? Because it is so hard to survive in Malawi, the Synod of Livingstonia makes loans to women to help them start small businesses. The women sell sugar, vegetables, corn, clothing, and other items. They work together to encourage and help each other. They repay the money they have borrowed so that other women will get a loan to start businesses of their own. When you add it up, you see that by helping each other, help is multiplied!

Word of the Week

Liturgy

Liturgy means "the work of the people." It is the word we use to describe the things we do in worship. That makes our worship "the work of the people."

Through the Synod of Livingstonia, women receive loans to start businesses like this store.

What You Can Do

Find the page for Malawi in the *Mission Yearbook for Prayer & Study*. Choose three people from that page to pray for. Use your prayer beads to remind you to pray for them.

MISSION IN THE UNITED STATES
Presbytery of East Tennessee

For more than thirty years, the Morgan Scott Project has helped people in the hills of east Tennessee. The project helped people help themselves by meeting their basic needs. But when tornadoes roared through the hills and valleys, everything changed. Houses were destroyed. People didn't even have the most basic things. With the help of the Morgan Scott Project, people who endured the effects of the tornados are getting their needs met. And because they know they have help, they are not giving up. Volunteers are helping to build new homes, working together to build hope. Truckloads of furniture, food, and supplies are being delivered. The Presbytery of East Tennessee is helping with supplies, money, and volunteers. (Find this presbytery on the map on page 112.) Jill Potter, the director of the interdenominational Morgan Scott Project, says, "The most difficult things to replace are the small possessions that are normally used during the day. The lack of these small things makes the adjustment to new living arrangements more difficult." One item that has helped children is a gift of teddy bears that talk, sing, and recite a bedtime prayer, ending with "I love you!" With help and encouragement of people from nearby and far away, the Morgan Scott Project continues to care for its neighbors.

Jill Potter is the director of the Morgan Scott Project.

SCRIPTURE

"Whoever serves me must follow me, and where I am, there will my servant be also" (John 12:26).

Recipe
Green Bean Salad

Cooking in South Africa has been influenced by the Dutch and by immigrants from Indonesia and Java. Try this way of making green beans! Ask an adult in your family to help you prepare this yummy dish.

Ingredients
2 pounds fresh green beans, trimmed
1/2 cup olive oil
4 tbs. lemon or lime juice
1 tsp. salt
1/2 tsp. cracked pepper
1 cup sweet white onions, thinly sliced
1/4 cup sliced stuffed green olives

Cook the beans in a large pot of boiling water until tender. Drain well. In a large bowl, combine the oil, lemon or lime juice, salt, and pepper. Stir well. Add the onions, green olives, and hot beans and toss until coated. Serve immediately.

Look in the 2004 Mission Yearbook *for Prayer & Study to find the Synod of the Living Waters page. Where in the world does the synod help provide clean water in partnership with other denominations?*

MISSION AROUND THE WORLD

Lesotho

Look at the map of Africa on page 110. Find South Africa. Then see if you can find Lesotho. Do you see it, surrounded by South Africa? Lesotho is known as the mountain kingdom. It is one of five southern African countries hardest hit by food shortages in 2002–2003. There are groups giving food, but often the groups don't consider the reasons people don't have enough to eat. In Lesotho, Kopano ke Matla Toantšong ea Bofuma (that means "Strength through Unity Fighting Poverty") is part of the Joining Hands Against Hunger Network. Members look for the causes of poverty and hunger and then work together to help fix the causes. They share information and experiences and stand up for those who don't have enough to eat. They can help people change the things that cause famine, hunger, and poverty. Mission co-workers Bob and Samantha Franklin work with the Joining Hands Against Hunger Network.

Did You Know?

In Lesotho, summer starts in November and lasts until January. Winter is from May to July. So if you are going to Lesotho for *your* summer vacation, when will you go?

PRAYER

Hallelujah! God, your servants show your love by caring for the people in Lesotho and in the Presbytery of East Tennessee! Help me to learn how to serve others. Bless and keep those who are servant leaders, like your son Jesus, in whose name we pray. Amen.

Word of the Week
Servant

Jesus teaches us to be servants to each other. The elders in your church are servant leaders, those who lead by meeting the needs of others.

Giving What You Have

Be a secret servant. Each week for the next four weeks, be a servant to someone at home or school. Secretly do one of your sister's chores. Make your brother's bed in secret. Wash the dishes without being asked. Look around for the ways you can serve, and be a servant quietly, without expecting praise.

What You Can Do

Are you ever wasteful? Keep an eye on yourself this week and look for the ways in which you might be wasting precious resources like water, paper, and food. Then work on finding ways to be less wasteful.

MISSION IN THE UNITED STATES

Presbytery of Memphis

Tennessee, Arkansas, Missouri

One child at a time. When the presbytery's Committee on Mission and Social Witness decided to focus its resources, its members decided to make a difference one child at a time. The committee gives grants to small churches that help children and youth. A grant helps First Presbyterian Church in Caruthersville, Missouri, give 200 children a summer camp experience. A grant to Bethel Presbyterian Church in downtown Memphis supports a program to educate youth and their parents about such issues as peer pressure and self-esteem. At the Liberation Church

SCRIPTURE

He went into all the region around the Jordan, proclaiming a baptism of repentance for the forgiveness of sins (Luke 3:3).

in Memphis, a grant helps create a safe, Christian environment for children to learn conflict resolution, build self-esteem, visit the library, and study the Bible. Children and youth can learn foreign languages, swim, make pottery, and enjoy music through a grant at rural LaGrange Presbyterian Church. Grace Presbyterian Church in Dyersburg, Tennessee, provides summer child care. With grants to churches, the Presbytery of Memphis is sharing God's love: one child at a time. Find the Presbytery of Memphis on the map on page 112.

Word Puzzle: Words in the Water

Each fish contains a scrambled word. Unscramble the letters inside each fish, then arrange the words to form a sentence found in A Brief Statement of Faith. Hint: The last word is baptism.

Hint: Start with this fish.

_____ _____ _____ _____ _____ _____ _____ _____ _____.

Answer: God claims us in the waters of baptism.

MISSION AROUND THE WORLD

Uganda

Our mission co-worker in Uganda, Ruth Montgomery, recently received a package from the United States. (Find Uganda on the map on page 110.) Here is a part of Ruth's thank-you letter.

Hi everybody,

Thank you for the things you have sent. A beautiful cobalt blue pen with gold trim was offered to the first student who completed twenty long-multiplication problems. The competition was intense, but Nampiima Christine was the champion. All the students who corrected their papers received black pens. Boy, did they love math that day! We received the soccer balls, thankfully! We are having a six-school tournament today, and our only soccer ball before you sent the new ones would have had to be blown up several times during each game. Our library has gone from thirteen books to about 150, including books and great animal magazines from so many people that I've lost track. Imagine children looking at books like they want to eat them. Please keep sending books!

Love,
Ruth

PRAYER

Find one of your favorite books. Sit quietly and read. After a while, stop and think of all the things you have to be thankful for: the book that you have, the fact that you can read when some children have not yet learned to read, the place you are. Thank God for them and many other ways you are blessed.

What You Can Do

Start a book drive to send books to a local group that works with children and would like more books. Or you can call the People in Mutual Mission office in the Worldwide Ministries Division at the PC(USA) Center in Louisville, Kentucky, 1-888-728-7228, ext. 5612. Ask church members to donate copies of their favorite children's books.

Did You Know?

When the United Presbyterian Church in the United States of America and the Presbyterian Church in the United States joined together in 1983 to form the Presbyterian Church (U.S.A.), a new statement of faith was written. It's called A Brief Statement of Faith. You can find it in the PC(USA)'s *Book of Confessions*.

Giving What You Have

Is there someone in your church, neighborhood, or family whom you could read to? Offer to read a favorite book to that person.

Word of the Week: Baptism

Baptism is an outward sign of being part of God's family. When we baptize children, we make a promise to teach them about God's love.

Did You Know?

Presbyterians have two sacraments—one is baptism. Do you know what the other sacrament is?

MISSION IN THE UNITED STATES
Presbytery of Great Rivers
Illinois

How far is it from the Presbytery of Great Rivers in Illinois to the Assu Valley in Northeast Brazil? Look at the map on page 112 and find the Presbytery of Great Rivers, then find Brazil on the map on page 110. See if you can estimate the distance. Even though they are very far apart, the Presbyteries of Great Rivers and Northeast Brazil have been partners for six years. Ten visitors from Brazil have come to visit the United States, and in 2003 two groups from the United States traveled to Brazil.

The partnership helps with projects like starting small businesses and building church buildings that provide jobs, job training, and day care programs. One-fourth of all the shared mission support dollars in the Presbytery of Great Rivers are used to fund the International Partnership activities with Brazil.

Brazilian mission workers from Assu Valley lead the worship service at Second Presbyterian Church, Bloomington, Illinois.

Word of the Week

Forgiveness

When Jesus forgives us, all our sins are forgotten! That's forgiving AND forgetting!

SCRIPTURE

When he saw their faith, he said, "Friend, your sins are forgiven you" (Luke 5:20).

Craft
Sun Catcher

Next week is when the Peacemaking Offering is collected. Prepare for Peacemaking and World Communion Sunday by making a sun catcher to hang in your window or to give to a friend.

Materials

1 overhead transparency sheet
permanent markers—black, red, blue (others colors if you want)

Draw the design on the transparency using the black marker. Fill in the spaces with the other colors. Use tape to put it on your window. See the sun shine through it!

Giving What You Have

Jesus said to forgive "seven times seventy" times. How many times is that? Save 70 cents to give to the Peacemaking Offering next week.

Did You Know?

In 2002, Presbyterian Disaster Assistance responded to disasters in 26 states in the United States and in 45 countries.

What You Can Do

Ask your pastor how you can help prepare for Peacemaking and World Communion Sunday. Maybe you can make the bread!

Did You Know?

Next week we celebrate World Communion Sunday. The Presbyterian Church started it back in 1936 with the idea that other denominations would join in. And they did! It's a day to remember that all over the world Christians are taking Communion in the name of Jesus. World Communion Sunday is always celebrated on the first Sunday in October. Many Presbyterian churches also collect the Peacemaking Offering on that Sunday.

PRAYER

This week, offer to pray before your family's evening meal. Thank God for the many gifts God has given you. Ask God's forgiveness for the things that you have done wrong. Ask God to bless the work of the Presbytery of Great Rivers and the country of Mozambique.

MISSION AROUND THE WORLD

Mozambique

Like Angola, Mozambique was once ruled by Portugal. After a seventeen-year civil war, the country finally stopped fighting in 1992. Mozambique has rich soil, so farming is one way the country can recover from the hard times. It could become the major food supplier for southern Africa. Presbyterian Disaster Assistance gave a grant to the Christian Council of Mozambique to buy seeds for 35,751 families in time for last year's planting season. The Presbyterian Church of Mozambique (IPM) has the help of PC(USA) mission co-workers Diane and Charles Wonnenberg. "We work with IPM in spreading the good news of Jesus Christ and offering abundant life through faith in God," write Charles and Diane. Find Mozambique on the map on page 110.

Peacemaking Offering

SCRIPTURE

And I will grant peace in the land . . . and no one shall make you afraid (Leviticus 26:6).

MISSION IN THE UNITED STATES

Presbytery of Central Washington

Every Thursday during the summer the Campbell Farm, a Presbyterian mission station located on the Yakama Indian Reservation, becomes a safe and fun place for forty to fifty Native American and Hispanic children who come for a picnic barbeque. Children visit the pigs, chickens, ducks, geese, miniature horses, llamas, alpacas, rabbits, kittens, and puppies. In the children's garden they crawl though the cucumber tunnel, hide in the sunflower house and beanpole tent, and stuff themselves on raspberries.

Mission teams from across the country come to work at the Campbell Farm, and the Thursday barbeque is one of the main outreach activities in which they participate. Mission team members set up activity stations for outdoor games, arts and crafts, music, and drama. Throughout the evening there is time for piggyback rides and getting to know each other.

Everyone gathers together for the last part of Thursday's program. Children perform the biblical skit they worked on that day. Everyone sings "Jesus Loves Me" by popular demand of a few preschoolers who know it by heart and then "Nellie Campbell Had a Farm" in honor of the woman who donated the farm to the Presbyterian Church twenty-five years ago. The evening ends with a circle of prayers as children offer their simple thanks and concerns to God.

Peacemakers David Hacker and the Rev. Sheri Noah are the directors of the Campbell Farm.

A Creation Collage

Find a heavy piece of construction paper or a piece of cardboard. In your home or in the area outside your home, find things that represent those parts of God's world for which you are thankful. They may include leaves, stones, feathers—whatever speaks to you. Do not use anything living, though. Glue them to the paper or cardboard and decorate it. Share your creation collage with someone in your family or at your church.

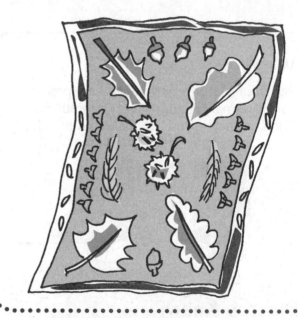

Did You Know?

Congregations and presbyteries or synods keep 25 percent of the Peacemaking Offering and use the money to care for other people and God's creation in many different ways in your community. If your congregation receives the Offering, find out how the funds received will be used.

MISSION AROUND THE WORLD

Iraq

Presbyterians have been at work in Iraq since 1839. Five Presbyterian churches exist in Iraq today. Along with the other people of Iraq, Christian churches and their members have suffered because of war and injustice. During the last war, Presbyterians in the United States prayed each day for those serving in our military and for the people of Iraq. After the war ended, U.S. Presbyterians provided food and medicine to those in need. Help was also provided as Iraqi Christians made a new start. Churches and presbyteries gave a share of their Peacemaking Offering to a special fund that was used to teach new pastors, provide Sunday school material, rebuild damaged buildings, aid and train doctors and nurses, and start new churches. Find Iraq on the map on page 110.

Children at the Assyrian Evangelical Church in Bagdad, Iraq, sing during morning worship.

PRAYER

Creator God, you looked at everything you made and called it good. We thank you for the air we breathe, the food we eat, the water we drink. We pray that this abundance you have given us may be shared with our brothers and sisters around the world. Help us to care for your creation and to be mindful of the needs of generations to come. We ask these things in the name of your son, Jesus Christ, who lives and reigns with you, in the unity of your Spirit. Amen.

Word of the Week

Ecojustice

Ecojustice is caring for God's world and for other people. It means working to protect the air, the water, and all living things. It involves working for a world of peace in which all people have enough to live healthy lives.

What You Can Do

The United Nations Children's Fund (UNICEF) provides children around the world with lifesaving medicine, proper nutrition, clean water, education, and emergency relief. It sponsors a Trick-or-Treat for UNICEF campaign each year through which children can raise money for other children. Instead of rushing from house to house for more candy, children collect donations for others in need. Please visit www.pcusa.org/peacemaking/un/unicef for more information about how you can collect funds for UNICEF this Halloween season.

Giving What You Have

Working to save the environment is part of good stewardship. One way we can be good stewards is to reduce our use of energy. Switching from regular light bulbs to compact fluorescent light bulbs (CFL) makes a big difference in the amount of energy we use. Talk to your family about changing the light bulbs in your home to CFLs.

Word of the Week

Home

Home is a place of safety, a sanctuary where you can rest and feel loved. Our heart's home is with God, and God will always take us in.

MISSION IN THE UNITED STATES

Midwest Hanmi Presbytery

Nongeographic

Kwangsu finished college, but he couldn't find work. So this immigrant from Korea decided to open a store with his small savings. He leased an old store in a run-down neighborhood in Chicago and sold mostly socks, gloves, hats, and other inexpensive clothes. He was able to live simply on income from the store. Then he began to feel God calling him to love the suffering neighbors who came to his store. At the age of fifty, he decided to go to school to become a pastor. Kwangsu is a friend to the homeless, lonely people, and troubled teens. He eats and prays with them and looks for new ways of expressing love for them. He helps them find a better life through prayer gatherings and worship services. Now he has a small church in his store called the House of Prayer Presbyterian Church. Kwangsu also teaches Bible on Wednesdays and Fridays. He asks for prayers that more people can be helped by God's love.

SCRIPTURE

"Return to your home, and declare how much God has done for you" (Luke 8:39).

Recipe

Kimchi (Pickled Cabbage)

Makes 1 gallon
Kimchi is a very popular and nutritious Korean dish. It requires no cooking. Could you use a gallon or so? Here's how to make it.

Ingredients

3 medium napa (Chinese) cabbages
1/2 cup salt
2 medium white radishes, peeled and shredded
1/3 cup red pepper powder
1 tbs. sugar
2 cloves garlic, chopped
2 tsp. ginger root, chopped
5 green onions, sliced

Remove cabbages' outer leaves and roots. Cut the cabbage into 1 1/2-inch squares. Place the cabbage in a large container and sprinkle with salt. Set aside for 2 or more hours or until the cabbage becomes soft. Rinse the pickled cabbage with water at least once and drain. Add the rest of the ingredients and mix well. Place the cabbage in a gallon-sized glass (not plastic) jar and leave in a cool place for at least 3 days or until it ferments and tastes a little sour. Then store it in the refrigerator (which will stop the fermentation). Kimchi will last in the refrigerator for two months.

CABBAGE

Giving What You Have

How many years have you lived where you live now? For each year, put 10 cents into the offering plate on Sunday.

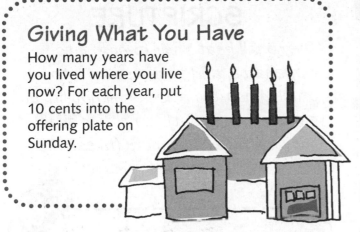

Did You Know?

Botswana and South Africa are two of the countries hardest hit by the worldwide HIV/AIDS epidemic. At the end of 2002 an estimated 330,000 people were living with HIV in Botswana with a total population of 1.6 million. In South Africa, over 5 million people are HIV positive, and nearly 20 percent of the 15–49-year-old population have HIV.

What You Can Do

Can you reach out to people with AIDS in your community? One group of children fixed plates of food from church potluck dinners, then took them to a nearby AIDS support center for people who were sick. What can you do?

PRAYER

God, you have done so much for us! We know you are with us even in the worst of times. You sent Jesus to heal the sick and your Holy Spirit to comfort us when we suffer. Help us to share your love with others. Give your hope to those who suffer and to those who help them in Botswana. We ask this in Jesus' name. Amen.

MISSION AROUND THE WORLD

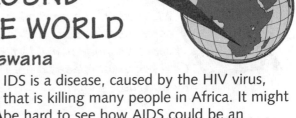

Botswana

AIDS is a disease, caused by the HIV virus, that is killing many people in Africa. It might be hard to see how AIDS could be an opportunity for sharing Christ's love. But it would be easy to see if you knew Mary and her friends at Home-Based Care Group ministries in Gaborone, Botswana. (Can you find Botswana on the map on page 110?) Mary and her friends visit the people sick with AIDS. They talk with them, listen to them, pray together, and sometimes share a song. They change their bedding and help with the laundry and preparing meals. They also talk with their family members and encourage them not to lose hope. Mary and her friends are messengers of the boundless love of Christ that helps us to see hope against all odds. For more information on the global HIV/AIDS crisis see www.churchworldservice.org.

photo by Andre J. Smith, courtesy of Church World Service

Bongi and her sisters at Sinikithemba Center in Durban, South Africa, are skilled in traditional Zulu beadwork. The beaded AIDS ribbon shown on this page is an example of their skill.

Did You Know?

The Presbyterian Church has been in mission service around the world since 1833.

SCRIPTURE

They shall beat their swords into plowshares, and their spears into pruning hooks; nation shall not lift up sword against nation, neither shall they learn war any more (Micah 4:3).

Word of the Week — Promise

When you make a promise to someone it is a good idea to keep it because it builds trust! God keeps promises to us. That's why we trust in God.

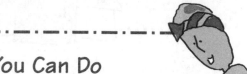

What You Can Do

Do you know the good news of God's great promises to you? Be a mission worker and share the good news with a friend.

Word Puzzle: Peace Promise

Find and circle in the puzzle all the words listed below. Words can go up, down, backward, and diagonally. When you are finished, write the letters remaining in the first 4 rows plus the first letter in row 5 in the spaces under the words. They will spell out a special message.

T	H	C	E	Y	N	W	S	H	A	L	L	B	A	E
A	T	H	T	H	A	E	O	E	I	R	S	W	L	O
R	D	I	S	G	I	I	N	R	C	T	O	P	O	L
O	W	L	O	S	R	H	F	M	S	A	A	R	G	E
S	F	D	E	W	E	D	R	Y	I	H	E	K	N	G
H	B	R	Y	J	T	A	I	T	X	S	I	P	A	O
L	A	E	A	J	Y	U	E	E	F	Y	S	P	W	O
C	P	N	C	T	B	B	N	S	P	I	R	I	T	D
H	M	J	Y	A	S	J	D	E	V	O	L	C	O	E
U	I	I	D	C	E	C	S	G	O	S	P	E	L	N
R	Z	M	C	P	R	O	P	H	E	C	Y	B	S	K
C	O	Y	Z	A	P	E	P	O	H	F	I	U	O	S
H	N	E	W	S	H	P	X	G	R	B	S	T	L	R
O	V	F	U	H	R	U	W	W	T	E	E	Z	U	G
D	A	L	O	U	M	X	Z	Q	J	B	Y	P	P	C

ANGOLA	BIBLE	CARE	CHILDREN	CHURCH
FRIENDS	GOD	GOOD	GOSPEL	HOPE
JESUS	LOVE	MICAH	MISSION	NEWS
PEACE	PRESBYTERIAN	PROPHECY	SPIRIT	WORSHIP

_ _ _ _ _   _ _ _ _ _   _ _ _ _

_ _ _ _ _ _ _ _ _ _ _ _ _ .

(For help, look at the Scripture verse for this week.)

MISSION AROUND THE WORLD

Angola

When the Portuguese made a part of southwest Africa a colony, they named it after the title of the local ruler, *ngola*. So the country was called Angola. (Find Angola on the map on page 110.) In 1975, when Angola became independent from Portugal, a civil war that lasted for years broke out. In 2002 the warring groups finally signed a peace agreement. But much needed to be done. Four million people had left their homes. Many families lived in the wilderness for years to escape the fighting. They scavenged for food and had no health care, education, or other services. Many were injured by land mines left by the war. Presbyterian Disaster Assistance provided money to help with health services, farming, water and sanitation programs, and food. They also taught people about the dangers of land mines. Maybe now the people of Angola can find out what it is like to live in peace.

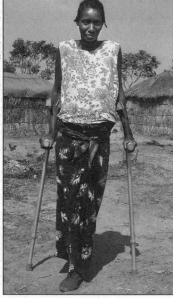

photo by Paul Jeffrey/ACT

Linda Mosango is one of more than 86,000 people injured by land mines in Angola.

Giving What You Have

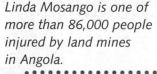

Keeping a promise you have made to someone is a good way to give. Make a promise to help someone this week and keep it!

PRAYER

God, your word promises us peace. Give your peace to the people of Angola. Thank you for the work of the Presbytery of Blackhawk. Let your peace and good news be spread everywhere, in the name of your child, Jesus. Amen.

MISSION IN THE UNITED STATES

Presbytery of Blackhawk

Illinois

Have you ever heard those jokes about bad news and good news? Usually they start, "There's good news and there's bad news." At Apple River Presbyterian Church in rural Illinois, there's just good news! The church people decided they had to do something different. They talked it over and concluded that they needed to reach out to children. The result was the Good News Club.

The Good News Club is an after-school program for grade-school children. Every Wednesday, kids come for Bible study, snacks, and crafts. Alvin Sigafus teaches the children about prayer. Alvin says the boys and girls are sometimes "a little rowdy." For many of the children this has been their first opportunity to hear the good news of God's love for them. There's more good news: Apple River Church, with only about twenty in worship each week, has about eighteen students in the club! They hope to sponsor ten to twelve children for the presbytery's summer camp. And that is good news! Find the Presbytery of Blackhawk on the map on page 112.

GOOD NEWS CLUB

MISSION IN THE UNITED STATES

Presbytery of the John Knox

Iowa, Minnesota, Wisconsin

Bangor is a small, pretty town in the rolling hills of western Wisconsin. Bangor Presbyterian Church has served the community and Christ's kingdom since 1872.

The church has a partnership with the Maasai people of Kenya, Africa. The church members were thrilled when their church was chosen to host some Maasai visitors. They raised $15,000 to purchase a truck for a Kenyan pastor who oversees twenty-nine churches! Now they assemble tote bags containing such items as medicines, hats, pencils, sunglasses, bandages, and other needed items. Elder Linda Masey, a volunteer in mission, takes the totes to Kenya. Jesus said, "For where your treasure is, there will your heart be also" (Luke 12:34). The growing mission work of Bangor Presbyterian Church has given their members a bigger heart, a heart that's supporting life, service, and mission at home and abroad. Find the Presbytery of the John Knox on the map on page 112.

Members of Bangor Presbyterian Church do mission work among Kenya's Maasai people.

What does Bangor Presbyterian Church in Bangor, Wisconsin, collect for the Ronald McDonald House? For the answer look in the Mission Yearbook for Prayer & Study on the page about the Presbytery of the John Knox.

SCRIPTURE

Satisfy us in the morning with your steadfast love, so that we may rejoice and be glad all our days (Psalm 90:14).

Craft

Kenya's flag is composed of black, red, white, and green stripes with a Maasai shield in the center. The shield stands for defense of the country. The colors mean something, too—for instance, the green stands for growth. What would your personal flag look like? What colors would you use, and what pictures would stand for you? Create your own flag and display it in your room. Use construction paper, markers, stickers, and crayons to make the flag of you!

Word of the Week

Compassion

Compassion means to care about someone else's distress and to have the desire to help. Mission is all about compassion and love.

MISSION AROUND THE WORLD

Kenya

If you went to Rubate College in East Africa to prepare for a career, you would be preparing twice. You would learn about education and teaching. You would also learn about mission. That's because you would get to be a volunteer Sunday school teacher in the nearby churches. Some of the churches are several miles from the college. Through the dry, hot season as well as the rainy, muddy season, you might walk and sometimes go by bicycle to teach young children about Jesus.

The Presbyterian Women Thank Offering (including Health Ministries) provided funds to support a women's program in eastern Kenya in 2000. They helped buy dairy cows for Kenyan women. Before, the women could sometimes find work as field hands, but they did not earn enough to support their families. Two years later, the women's program provided a stable source of income for more than twenty-five women through sales of cow's milk. Plus, good milk to drink has meant better health for the families. An additional blessing of this ministry is that it reproduces itself. When the cows give birth, women can provide calves to other women. Then their lives and the lives of other women and children can also be improved. Find Kenya on the map on page 110.

Giving What You Have

How many quarts of milk are in your house? (Four quarts make one gallon.) For each quart of milk save 10 cents to give to the Thank Offering.

PRAYER

God, we praise you for the love and compassion of the people of Kenya and the churches of the Presbytery of the John Knox. Help me to be more compassionate and love to do your work wherever I go. In Jesus' name. Amen.

What You Can Do

Ask the members of Presbyterian Women at your church how you can give to the Thank Offering (including Health Ministries). Ask them what they use the money for.

Did You Know?

After the attacks of September 11, 2001, the Maasai people of Kenya wanted to give a gift to the United States to help us feel better. Because their cattle are the most important treasure the Maasai people have, they gave a gift of cattle to the United States. They gave a gift of love and compassion.

MISSION IN THE UNITED STATES

The Presbytery of Des Moines

Iowa

Can you imagine living in a refugee camp for seven years—away from your home, your friends, and your family? In the spring of 2002, Union Park Presbyterian Church in Des Moines decided to sponsor a Bosnian refugee family. They worked together to find housing, furniture, clothing, and food for the family. The Veletic family (dad Dragan, mom Dragica, and teenage sons Goran and Stojan) arrived in August, after spending seven years in a refugee camp. There was a long list of things for church members to do for the family: find jobs for the parents, enroll the boys in school, get Social Security cards, get drivers' licenses, open bank accounts, and provide transportation. When Dragan needed tools for his mechanic's job, members raised about $1,500 within a week to purchase the tools. They brought decorations for the family's first Christmas tree in seven years. They gave the family a computer and loaned them a car. All who work with the Veletic family feel blessed. During such a huge adjustment to a new country and a new place the family has kept a sense of humor. Union Park is a better church for knowing such an extraordinary family who has traveled so far to a new home. The church's members have given generously of themselves and in sharing have become better disciples of Christ.

Find Iowa and the Presbytery of Des Moines on the map on page 112.

SCRIPTURE

"Indeed, some are last who will be first, and some are first who will be last" (Luke 13:30).

Recipe

Banjaluka's Chevap (Beef Stew)

This is a recipe that comes from Bosnia and Herzegovina. Remember to ask for help when using the stove.

Ingredients

1 1/2 lbs. stew meat (cut into 1-inch cubes)
1/2 cup flour
1 tbs. sugar
1/4 cup vegetable oil
4 cups water
1 8-oz. can tomato sauce
1/2 tsp. crushed red pepper
2 cups frozen vegetables
salt (to taste)

Put the flour and sugar into a sealable plastic bag and mix together well. Put the stew meat into the bag and shake until the meat is coated with the flour and sugar mixture. Heat the vegetable oil in a large saucepan or soup pot on medium high heat. When the oil is hot, add the coated stew meat and flour. Brown the meat. After the meat chunks are brown, add water and tomato sauce. Let simmer on medium heat for 30 minutes, then add 2 cups of frozen mixed vegetables, red pepper, and salt to taste. Serve with bread or mashed potatoes.

MISSION AROUND THE WORLD

Cameroon

Concerned women and men in the Fako North and South Presbyteries of the Presbyterian Church of Cameroon felt the need for better education for girls. They began to raise money to achieve their dream. Girls began their studies in borrowed buildings. Meanwhile, the churches prepared plans for a school building and raised money. The PC(USA) has also helped. The Presbyterian Girls' Secondary School in Limbe has grown from forty-two students in the first year to 578 students in the fourth year. As the work continues, some girls have already moved to the new school building. It is on the slope of Mt. Cameroon and has a distant view of the ocean. The church also operates a scholarship program. That means that students who work hard at school can still attend even though they can't afford to pay the school fees. Find Cameroon on the map on page 110.

Students from the Presbyterian Girl's School in Limbe greet the sun together before attending classes.

Did You Know?

Limbe, in Cameroon, is known for its black sand beaches, the result of volcanic activity from Mt. Cameroon.

PRAYER

God, help me learn to put others first, as mission workers have done in Cameroon and in the Presbytery of Des Moines. Give me humility to serve you by serving others. In Jesus' name. Amen.

Word of the Week

Humility

Humility means to be modest and to practice putting others before yourself. It is a trait that Christ showed. Mission workers show humility when they serve others.

What You Can Do

In Cameroon and in Des Moines, Presbyterians are helping others get good starts in school and in a new country. Think about the people who have helped you in school or during changes in your life. Write a short note to tell them how they helped you and say thanks to them.

THANK YOU!

Thanks for bringing music to my life.

Giving What You Have

Make the Banjaluka's chevap (beef stew) and take it to someone who would appreciate it—perhaps an older person in your congregation who can't get out or someone who is sick.

SCRIPTURE

But be doers of the word, and not merely hearers who deceive themselves (James 1:22).

Giving What You Have

How many Spanish words do you know? Add 5 cents to the church offering plate on Sunday for each one. If you know a lot of Spanish words, give 5 cents for every Spanish word in the puzzle below.

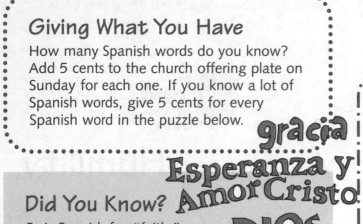

Did You Know?

Fe is Spanish for "faith."

What You Can Do

How can you put love into action? This week think of two people you love and care about. Secretly do one nice thing for each of them. Don't let them know it was you!

Word Puzzle

Bilingual Word Wrap

In this puzzle are words in Spanish and English. Find the words on the list at the starting numbers and shade them in. The first list of words is in capital letters. If you shade the words that are in capitals in one color, and the words using lowercase letters in another color, you will find a new word is outlined in the puzzle. We've shaded in one word to get you started.

	1	2	3	4	5	6	7	8	9	10	11	12
I	F	A	I	T	l	u	z	O	S	G	R	d
II	P	O	H	H	s	o	n	I	E	C	A	o
III	E	s	p	i	r	i	t	D	e	l	c	a
IV	E	S	P	E	h	a	c	L	O	V	E	r
V	Z	N	A	R	i	m	e	C	A	R	G	i
VI	A	r	g	a	l	c	r	I	p	s	e	m
VII	G	o	r	h	c	s	i	A	i	r	i	t
VIII	O	s	i	s	t	t	o	A	M	O	R	u

FAITH (1, I)	AMOR (8, VIII)	cristo (6, VI)	miracle (12, VI)
HOPE (3, II)	GRACE (10, I)	christ (5, VII)	son (5, II)
ESPERANZA (1, IV)	DIOS (8, III)	milagros (6, V)	luz (5, I)
GO (1, VII)	LOVE (8, IV)	hace (5, IV)	do (12, I)
GRACIA (11, V)	spirit (2, III)	espíritu (11, VI)	

Word of the Week

Action

God asks us to be more than hearers; God asks us to be doers! Mission is love in action.

MISSION IN THE UNITED STATES

Homestead Presbytery

Nebraska

"Cristo te ama." That's the way they say "Jesus loves you" in . . . Nebraska! Most people think of Czechs, Germans, beef, and football when they think of Nebraska. But Hispanics, tacos, and soccer have become important parts of "the good life" in Nebraska. Homestead Presbytery formed a Hispanic/Latino Commission to explore ways to welcome Spanish-speaking people who have come to Nebraska from the south and southwestern parts of the United States. They also come from Mexico, Guatemala, Honduras, El Salvador, Peru, Colombia, Paraguay, and Cuba. They are coming to Nebraska for jobs, mainly in meat-packing plants. They come in hopes of making a better life for themselves and their children. The Rev. Juventino "Tino" Naranjo leads the Fe, Esperanza y Amor ("faith, hope, and love") Bilingual Ministries. He travels to cities and small towns to minister to people in Spanish.

As Homestead Presbytery starts new ministries and continues to support old ones, it shares the promise of the apostle Paul that "you know that your labor in the Lord is not in vain" (1 Corinthians 15:58). Find Homestead Presbytery on the map on page 112.

Did You Know?

About 27 million people in the United States today are from Spanish-speaking countries.

MISSION AROUND THE WORLD

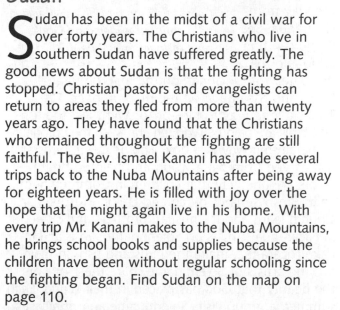

Sudan

Sudan has been in the midst of a civil war for over forty years. The Christians who live in southern Sudan have suffered greatly. The good news about Sudan is that the fighting has stopped. Christian pastors and evangelists can return to areas they fled from more than twenty years ago. They have found that the Christians who remained throughout the fighting are still faithful. The Rev. Ismael Kanani has made several trips back to the Nuba Mountains after being away for eighteen years. He is filled with joy over the hope that he might again live in his home. With every trip Mr. Kanani makes to the Nuba Mountains, he brings school books and supplies because the children have been without regular schooling since the fighting began. Find Sudan on the map on page 110.

The Rev. Fahed Abu-Akel, moderator of the 214th General Assembly (2002), visits with children in a refugee camp in Sudan.

MISSION IN THE UNITED STATES
Presbytery of Cincinnati
Ohio

Carved fish and birds from Nicaragua help children understand God's plan of love among people.

"Fish gotta swim, birds gotta fly . . . " That's a line from an old song. Some fish and birds come to the Presbytery of Cincinnati all the way from Nicaragua. See if you can find Ohio and the Presbytery of Cincinnati on the map on page 112. Now, find Nicaragua on the map on page 110. That's a long way to fly—or to swim! But the fish and birds are painted wooden crafts, so they probably come all that way in a box. The beautiful birds and fish carved from balsa wood and painted bright colors are one way that children in Community of Faith Presbyterian Church and Union Presbyterian Church learn about Christian brothers and sisters in Nicaragua. Artists on Solentiname, an island in Lake Nicaragua, make the birds and fish. In their art, the artists of Solentiname share their love of the beauty that God has placed in their world. Each summer, a group visits Solentiname and purchases the carved birds and fish, paintings, and pottery. Back home, they sell the artwork at church festivals. Then they send the money back to Nicaragua. The Nicaraguans use the money to support projects that they plan and carry out themselves.

Word of the Week

Sovereign

A sovereign is one who rules, like a king or queen. God is sovereign over all creation.

SCRIPTURE

From the rising of the sun to its setting my name is great among the nations (Malachi 1:11).

Craft
Fabric Art

You can make a fabric wall hanging or a tote bag.

Materials

1 or 2 squares of cloth, 12" x 12"
scraps of cloth, beads, sequins
old jewelry, buttons
12-inch piece of cord or yarn

You will need two squares if you are making a tote bag. The square is the background for your art. Use brightly colored fabric scraps to make a design. Cut out bird or fish shapes. Glue them to the background. Glue on beads, sequins, or smaller pieces of cloth. You can use white glue, but if you plan to wash your creation, use fabric glue so it will stay together. If you are making a tote bag, sew or staple the two pieces together on three sides, leaving the top open. If you know how to sew, stitch on the cord or yarn to make a hanger or handles. If you don't sew, use a stapler to attach the cord or yarn.

MISSION AROUND THE WORLD

Ghana

One of the church's ministries in Ghana is the Presbyterian Women's Vocational Institute. Located in Begoro in southern Ghana, this Christian school teaches skills to girls and women so that they can get good jobs in Begoro. Now there is a special sewing program called Begoro Maid. This program hires the women who graduate from fashion classes to sew garments and handicrafts for sale in Ghana and throughout the world. The young women gain more sewing skills, and they learn accounting, purchasing, and marketing. After they have been through the training they may even start their own businesses.

In 2001 Begoro Maid received a grant from the Presbyterian Women's Thank Offering (including Health Ministries) to expand its factory space so it could add more staff members and students. The women of Begoro Maid sewed 1,500 of the tote bags that were given to participants at the 2003 Presbyterian Women's Gathering. Find Ghana on the map on page 110.

What You Can Do

There are lots of stores and shops that sell crafts made by people in countries like Nicaragua and Ghana. When you shop for arts and crafts, look for stores like SERRV International, Peacecraft, or Ten Thousand Villages. At these stores, the money from the sale of the arts and crafts helps people who make the crafts make their lives better.

Did You Know?

More than 100 presbyteries in the PC(USA) have made special partnerships with churches on other continents. These churches in other countries are called partner churches. Ask your pastor or your parents if your church has a partner church overseas.

PRAYER

God our Sovereign, we praise you for the work of the churches in Cincinnati and in Ghana that helps people use their talents to make our world better. Help us to care and pay attention to the things we buy, so that we are making good choices. In Jesus' name. Amen.

Poem
Hands

Swimming fish with carved fins,
Bright in your dark hands
As you carved and painted,
Lovingly shaped until it swam
Lightly into my hands.
Soaring bird with colored wings
Brilliant feathered,
Green, orange, red, blue
Flying from your fingers
To my small open hands.
God's hands hold us all,
Little fish, bright bird, artist, and me:
Joining us in love and in the
Shining colors of wriggling wooden fish
And fluttering wings of painted birds.

—by Christina Berry. Used with permission.

Giving What You Have

Count the number of different kinds of birds and fish you see this week. For each kind put 5 cents in the offering plate on Sunday. If you don't see any birds or fish, put 25 cents in the church offering plate on Sunday.

MISSION IN THE UNITED STATES

Presbytery of Detroit

Michigan

Check out this letter from the Presbytery of Detroit! (First, find where the presbytery is on the map on page 112.)

Dear Children's Mission Yearbook:

We like mission projects that help kids. Well, sure! We're kids. We like kids. We took crayons and markers donated from our town's early childhood center, added stickers, paper, a handmade coloring book, notecards, envelopes, and stamps and made Art Kits. On one notecard in the bag, we wrote our own note to its new owner: "Hi! Have fun with this stuff! I'm thinking about YOU." At the time, we had a food bank in the basement of our church and lots of the bags went there, but more went to our county's shelter for victims of abuse, and still more went to a soup kitchen in downtown Detroit.

Empty Stockings challenged our members to fill 150 red Christmas stockings! We filled 150 because our church is 150 years old this year. We gave them to our members on two Sundays. Three weeks later people returned them filled with goodies for babies, elementary-age kids, teens, and senior citizens. The kids said they had a hard time picking out things somebody might like, while deciding what they could afford and—sometimes—what would fit! You can't put a hula hoop in a fuzzy red sock!

You can tell these projects are fun for us. We also pray about them and for the people they will reach. We want kids to feel God in their lives, because God made each one of them and loves them more than we can know. It's part of our mission statement: Love God, Love One Another, Reach Out. Next, we're having a 21 Bun Salute! Do you think we'll reach our goal of sending 21 rabbits across the ocean?

SCRIPTURE

Do you not know that you are God's temple and that God's Spirit dwells in you? (1 Corinthians 3:16).

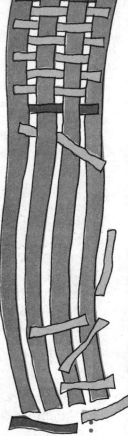

Craft

Advent Calendar

The season of Advent begins next Sunday, November 28. This year make a weaving.

Materials

construction paper (4 sheets each of 2 colors, and 1 sheet of a third color)
scissors   tape
markers   ruler

Cut 3 of the first colored sheets lengthwise into 2-inch wide strips that are about 11 inches long. Tape sets of 3 strips together at the ends to make four 30-inch long lengths. Using the same color of paper, cut 2 more strips that are 1 inch wide and 11 inches long. Lay the 4 long strips side by side and tape the 4 ends to one of the shorter strips. Do the same with the other 4 ends. Use tape to hang the long strips up on the wall. Cut the 5 remaining sheets into strips of paper about 1 inch wide and 11 inches long. There will be 24 of one color and 4 of the last color.

Starting on Sunday, November 28, pick out 1 of the 4 strips you have cut. Write your prayers for Advent on it, then weave it through the long strips, as close to the top as you can. Use tape to keep it in place. For Monday through Saturday, do the same with one of the 24 strips of paper. You can draw symbols or write prayers and songs on the strips. Use the 4 strips for the 4 Sundays of Advent, and the other 24 for the weekdays and Saturdays. When Christmas comes you will have a peace weaving to display or use on the table.

MISSION AROUND THE WORLD

Rwanda

Rwanda has been called "the country of a thousand hills and a million graves." If you read the *2003 Children's Mission Yearbook*, you may remember that for many years Rwanda was not a good or safe place to be. Two groups of people, called Hutus and Tutsis, were in a terrible conflict. The Hutus killed 800,000 Tutsis. Then the Tutsis fought back, and about two million Hutus fled to other countries. The genocide (that word means "killing a race of people") changed the country. This year marks the tenth anniversary of the genocide that claimed the lives of an estimated one million Rwandans. The Presbyterian Church of Rwanda is working to help many children left homeless by the war, genocide, diseases, and poverty.

Each summer high school students from the Presbyterian schools in Rwanda gather for a camp. The students play sports and enjoy cultural activities. They also talk about issues like AIDS, peace and social justice, and the role of youth in the church.

For orphans and children living on the streets members of the Presbyterian Church of Rwanda operate a number of centers. One center is the Presbyterian Center for the Love of Children, located in the capital, Kigali. There, students learn how to cook and cut hair. They make furniture from papier-mâché, and they beat and bend scrap metal into cooking tools, or create artistic wall decorations from a mixture of mud and grass. While the children learn and work, the leaders express their Christian love and hope for them. The children of Rwanda face a hard time, but God's love is present with them. Find Rwanda on the map on page 110.

Young people learn how to cook at the Presbyterian Center for the Love of Children.

PRAYER

God, please keep the children of Rwanda in your care, and give them a future of hope. Thank you for the work that people do in Rwanda and in the Presbytery of Detroit helping kids to feel God in their lives. Make me your temple, a place for your Spirit to live. In Jesus' name. Amen.

Word of the Week

Temple

A temple is a holy place. Our verse this week reminds us that we are holy places, because God's Spirit lives within us.

Giving What You Have

Count how many letters come to your home this week (you don't have to count magazines and advertisements) and save 5 cents for each one to give to the Christmas Joy Offering.

Did You Know?

In Rwanda, Hutu and Tutsi women are working together to make peace baskets. With the help of the United Nations, the women whose husbands were killed during the genocide have come together to weave traditional Rwandan baskets. When the baskets are sold, some of the money goes to the Global Peace Fund.

What You Can Do

Learn what projects your church will be doing this Christmas for people in need, and find out how you can be a part of helping others.

MISSION IN THE UNITED STATES

Presbytery of Lake Michigan

Michigan

Jesus said to go and make disciples of all nations. At the Presbytery of Lake Michigan, they are doing just that! The seventy churches in the presbytery are excited about their new church developments (NCD). They are starting four new and very different churches.

Pine Island Fellowship in Mattawan is small. The people worship in a college. Now they have to decide if they should charter as a small church with a part-time pastor or become part of another congregation. Even though the future feels uncertain, members of the fellowship are determined and optimistic that God has a plan for the congregation.

In East Lansing, the Korean Fellowship meets in the building of Peoples Presbyterian Church. That way, the Korean Fellowship can be close to the campus of Michigan State University, where there are many Korean students.

Caledonia Fellowship is a suburban NCD in a fast-growing town. The church meetings began in an elementary school. At first, the fellowship met once a month; now they meet every other week. Soon the fellowship hopes to have weekly worship, study, and fellowship.

Holland Probe in Holland, Michigan, is a whole new idea in ministry. It is a special kind of NCD for those who are in Generation-X (people between the ages of twenty and thirty-five—about 30 percent of the adult population). Many of the people in this age group have not been involved in any faith community. The new NCD is a fresh and exciting way to reach out to people who are seeking God's direction in their lives. Four NCDs for four places in four very different ways! God's love is abounding—and amazing! Find the Presbytery of Lake Michigan on the map on page 112.

Did You Know?

This is the first Sunday of Advent, the four weeks of preparing for Jesus' birth. Be sure to add to your Advent peace weaving every day this week.

SCRIPTURE

And may the Lord make you increase and abound in love for one another and for all, just as we abound in love for you (1 Thessalonians 3:12).

Word Puzzle

Light a Candle for Peace

Look up Psalm 122:8. Use the New Revised Standard Version. Write one word of the verse on each line of the candle. Then write the word of the corresponding number in the squares at the base of the candle. Use the message this week to help you prepare for Jesus to come.

MISSION AROUND THE WORLD

Equatorial Guinea

In the small country of Equatorial Guinea, the population is less than 500,000. Find it on the map on page 110. This country is about the size of the state of Maryland, and most of the people are Roman Catholic—about 90 percent. The tiny Reformed Church of Equatorial Guinea has a strong ministry in education. In the past, Protestant churches weren't allowed. Parents who wanted to send their children to the best schools sent them to schools run by the Roman Catholic Church. They had the best-educated teachers, and if your child did well, he or she might earn a *beca*—a scholarship—to study in Spain. But to attend one of those schools you had to be baptized a Catholic. This put Protestant parents in a bind. They could have their child baptized by the priest and claim to be Catholic so their child could enroll in a better school. Or they could send their child to an inferior school, even though they knew that a good education is very important. In 1980 Protestant schools and churches were allowed to exist again. The Reformed Church of Equatorial Guinea opened El Colegio Resurreccion in the city of Bata. Today the school has more than 800 students. Now children who are not Catholic can go to good schools and their parents know they are doing what is right.

New opportunities for learning are available to students in Equatorial Guinea.

PRAYER

God of abounding love, we see love in action in the new churches of the Presbytery of Lake Michigan, and in the school in Equatorial Guinea. Help us to abound in love—to always be acting and moving to share your love. In Jesus' name. Amen.

Giving What You Have

How many classes do you have at school? How many other lessons do you take (like piano, or trombone, or ocarina!)? Save 5 cents for every class and lesson you have to give to the Christmas Joy Offering that most churches collect the Sunday before Christmas.

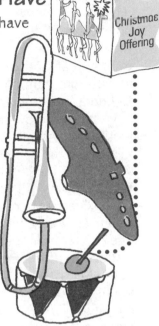

Word of the Week

Abound

To abound is to have lots and lots of something so you would not have to worry about running out. God's love is truly abounding!

What You Can Do

Ask your church school teacher to help your class find a project to help kids your age with school supplies or other needs for education.

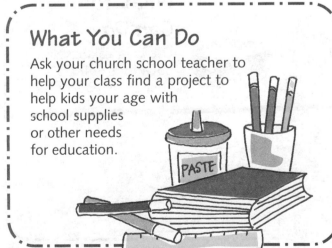

MISSION IN THE UNITED STATES

Presbytery of Central Washington

Community Presbyterian Church in Wapato is located on the Yakama Indian Reservation in the heart of the Presbytery of Central Washington. Find this presbytery on the map on page 112. The Wapato community is troubled by high levels of drug use, dropouts from school, and teenage suicide. Two years ago the elders began to pray that God would show them how to bring a youth program back to the church. They wanted to find a way to help young people. No one could have guessed how the program God had in mind would dramatically change both the ministry and mission of the church. One day Corey Greaves stopped by the church and shared his vision for youth ministry with the Rev. David Norwood. Corey Greaves became the youth director. Native American young people began to attend worship. They have responded to the teachings and instruction of the Christian faith and sixteen youth have been baptized. Discipleship classes are training young people to respond to the needs of the community. And families are coming to worship. Holding this program together is a joyful challenge according to Mr. Norwood. "It is easy to say that we support diversity, but when a large number of 'strangers' join together in community it challenges everyone's definition of who 'we' are and this challenge requires Christ's touch."

What You Can Do

Use your calabash bowl to tell others at your church about the mission work of the PC(USA) in Nigeria.

SCRIPTURE

Brothers and sisters, do not be weary in doing what is right (2 Thessalonians 3:13).

Craft

Papier-mâché Calabash Bowl

The Hausa people of Nigeria make bowls from calabash gourds. They use the bowls for food and for carrying milk. The outside of the calabash is decorated with designs.

Materials

medium-size plastic bowl (like an empty whipped topping tub)
newspaper
flour and water paste (see recipe)

Flour and water paste:

Make a paste of flour and water. Use 1/2 cup of flour to 1 cup of water. Add 1/4 teaspoon of salt. Stir well with a fork until you have a nice pasty mix with no lumps.

Spread some newspapers out to protect your work area. Tear other newspapers into strips. Turn the bowl upside down—you are using it as a form for the shape of your bowl. Drag the strips of paper through the paste and shape them over the bowl. Keep adding pasted strips and smoothing your bowl until you have a nice even shape. Let the bowl dry. Be patient; it may take a couple of days. When the bowl is dry, paint it light brown or tan and then use a black, fine-point permanent marker to add your designs. Traditional calabash bowl designs are simple lines, circles, curves, and zigzags. Use simple shapes to make interesting patterns.

Word of the Week

Strength

Strength means power of body, mind, or heart. We all gain strength from our learning and sharing with one another. God gives us the strength to do what is right, without growing weary.

Did You Know?

Nigeria has 645 Presbyterian churches and 250 ordained Presbyterian ministers. The Presbyterian Church of Nigeria, a partner of the PC(USA), has 123,919 members.

Giving What You Have

Diversity is what makes life interesting! Are there any Hausa, Yoruba, or other Nigerian people in your community? How about Yakama Indians? Find out about the many types of people in your community. There are men and women, boys and girls, people who have blue eyes, or brown . . . you get the idea! Each time you discover another interesting difference about someone in your community, save 5 cents to give to the Christmas Joy Offering, usually received the Sunday before Christmas.

What special day falls on December 10 and what document has these words: "All human beings are born free and equal in dignity and rights"? Look in the Mission Yearbook for Prayer & Study on page 346 for the answers!

PRAYER

Loving God, help us to be strong in you and to do what is right. Thank you for the ways your people are reaching out to those who need you in Wapato and in Nigeria. In Jesus' name. Amen.

MISSION AROUND THE WORLD

Nigeria

Get ready to think about fractions as we learn about Nigeria. In all of Africa there are 720 million people. Nigeria has a population of 120 million people. That makes it the most populous country in Africa. What fraction of Africans are Nigerian? Got it? 1/6 of all Africans are Nigerian.

Nigeria is a large country whose people are divided by people groups (tribes) and religion. More than 300 people groups are in Nigeria, the largest being the Hausa, who live mainly in the northern part of the country. The Yorubas are the second largest people group. They live mainly in the west and south. About 1/3 of the people are part of the Hausa and another people group, the Fulani. About 1/5 are Yoruba. And about 1/10 are Ibo.

About 1/2 of the people are Christian, and about 1/2 are Muslim. It is easy to see how there might be lots of disagreements about the way things should be. But no matter which group a Nigerian belongs to, God's love is for everyone—100 percent, or 6/6! Find Nigeria on the map on page 110.

The Rev. Benebo Fubara Fubara-Manuel is the principal clerk of the Presbyterian Church of Nigeria, our partner in Nigeria. His people group is the Kalabari.

MISSION IN THE UNITED STATES
Presbytery of Inland Northwest
Idaho, Washington

A family found the help they needed at Liberty Park Child Development Center in Spokane, Washington. Last year, this mom and her children didn't have a home to live in. For five months they stayed with different people and moved from house to house, from couch to couch. With some help the mom got a job and then was able to get an apartment. Since then she has received two promotions and the family has moved into its first house. Through five years of difficult times, Liberty Park was there to take care of the children. The mom could work without worrying about her children. She knew that her children were safe in a loving environment and having fun while she worked and planned for the future. Liberty Park Child Development Center is a Christian mission outreach center of the Presbytery of Inland Northwest. (Find this presbytery on the map on page 112.) Each day this center touches the lives of children and their families who are in need of safety, stability, and love. The center's motto is "Helping Families Help Themselves." They share Christ and his love and let everyone see God's love at work.

What You Can Do

Does your church have an annual craft bazaar or sale? Find out, and if they do, contribute some of your time or crafts.

Today!
Annual Church Bazaar

SCRIPTURE

I keep the LORD always before me; because [the LORD] is at my right hand, I shall not be moved (Psalm 16:8).

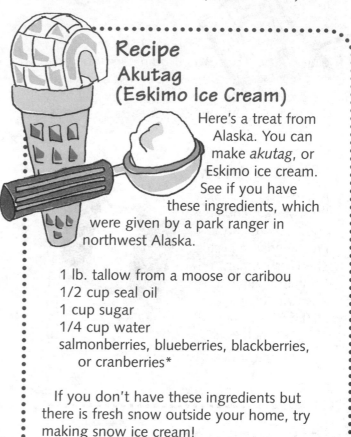

Recipe
Akutag (Eskimo Ice Cream)

Here's a treat from Alaska. You can make *akutag*, or Eskimo ice cream. See if you have these ingredients, which were given by a park ranger in northwest Alaska.

1 lb. tallow from a moose or caribou
1/2 cup seal oil
1 cup sugar
1/4 cup water
salmonberries, blueberries, blackberries, or cranberries*

If you don't have these ingredients but there is fresh snow outside your home, try making snow ice cream!

4 cups fresh snow (not packed down)
1 cup milk
1/2 tsp. vanilla
1/2 cup sugar

Mix the milk, vanilla, and sugar together in a bowl until you can't see the sugar. Then add snow a little at a time, stirring it in until it looks like ice cream. Eat it. You might need to keep a coat on.

If there isn't fresh snow on the ground, get an adult to take you to the store and buy your favorite flavor of ice cream!

*The ingredients for *akutag* are from *Plants That We Eat*, by Anore Jones and the Manillaq Association.

MISSION AROUND THE WORLD

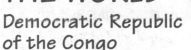

Democratic Republic of the Congo

In the Democratic Republic of the Congo, many women of the Presbyterian Community of Congo support their families and help the church. Some women raise and sell animals. Some dye and sell fabric. Others bake bread and cakes. Most, though, grow and sell a local food plant, manioc. The root is ground for meal and the leaves are steamed or boiled to eat. These projects all have two things in common. First, they are created and worked on collectively by a group of women. Second, the women commit to giving the first 20 percent of their profits to the church. The first 10 percent goes to the church in general and helps with its needs. The second 10 percent goes to the women's group in the church and their work. The women's group usually cares for the sick and provides food for those in need such as orphans, widows, and the elderly.

How much do these women make and give? One group of five women grew their crop of manioc last year. At the end of the year they had five dollars profit. Each woman took one dollar home. Each gave twenty cents to the church before using the rest. They had a good year.

Find the Democratic Republic of the Congo on the map on page 110.

Women are raising money for their families and their church by baking bread and cakes.

Find the Democratic Republic of the Congo on the map on page 110.

PRAYER

God, help the people who do mission work in the Presbytery of Inland Northwest and in the Democratic Republic of the Congo. Give them strength and energy to do your work. Help me, too, to do your work where I live. In Jesus' name. Amen.

Congolese women show rolls they have baked and have ready for sale.

Word of the Week Sharing

When you share your time to help take care of someone, whether it be a grandparent or a sister or a brother, you are sharing a special part of yourself with them. Mission is all about sharing with others at home and around the world.

Did You Know?

The practice of giving 10 percent back to God is called tithing. That is one way that people decide how much money to give the church.

Giving What You Have

How many dollars do you have right now? Save 10 percent of that for the Christmas Joy Offering.

Thank You

Christmas Joy Offering

Christmas Joy Offering

MISSION IN THE UNITED STATES
Presbytery of Dakota
Nongeographic

Jessica Charging Eagle is in Tempe, Arizona, at Cooke College, one of six colleges helped by the Christmas Joy Offering.

Jessica Charging Eagle is a member of the Cheyenne River Sioux tribe in South Dakota. Her grandfather once told her, "Don't let these hills be a fence that keeps you in. You must educate yourself and explore the world beyond these hills before you can bring your gifts back to your people." When she was young, she was more focused on getting a good job, because her family was poor. But when her grandfather died, at his funeral she remembered something he had told her. "He said one day I'd be a good student and a good writer," she remembers. "He told me I could do anything I put my mind to. I knew what he wanted me to do, and I decided to do it."

The next semester, she enrolled at Cook College and Theological School in Tempe, Arizona. After graduating, she plans to return to her hometown. "There are so many young people there who have nothing to do and have no hope," she says. "A lot of them get stuck watching television, lose touch with their own culture, and get into all kinds of problems. I want to help them find another way. I want to bring them stories of their history and a vision of hope."

The Christmas Joy Offering gives us a chance to share our gifts with students like Jessica as they find and develop their gifts so that they can share them with a larger world.

SCRIPTURE

"She will bear a son, and you are to name him Jesus, for he will save his people from their sins" (Matthew 1:21).

Activity
Maze
Help the light from the star find the way to the angel below.

Start Here

Word of the Week

Herald

A herald is one who announces or signals the beginning of something, or who brings a message. In the hymn "Hark the Herald Angels Sing," what do you think the angels are announcing?

Giving What You Have

How many countries have you heard about this year in this *Yearbook*? For each one, put a nickel in your Christmas Joy Offering coin bank. Do you know someone who is living in another country? For every country where you know someone, put in a quarter.

Did You Know?

Did you know that gifts to the Christmas Joy Offering enabled the Board of Pensions to help more than 550 families of church workers last year?

What You Can Do

Try to find out how people celebrate Christmas in another country. Has anyone in your congregation or your school ever lived in another country? Ask that person whether the citizens of that country have a long holiday from school like we do here. Do they eat special foods on Christmas Day? Do they have any customs like exchanging presents? Are there songs they like to sing around this time? Do they wear special clothes (like a red fuzzy hat with a white snowball on it)? If you don't know anyone who has lived in another country, during the Christmas season check your Internet browser to find sites that discuss Christmas customs in different countries.

PRAYER

Pray for the people you know who are living in other countries. Now pray for all the people you don't know who are living in the countries you've learned about this year. Ask God to help keep those you know and those you don't know safe from harm.

MISSION AROUND THE WORLD
Democratic Republic of the Congo

Ann Crane was a missionary in the Congo back in the 1960s. Her parents were missionaries there too, and she was actually born there, in a town called Luebo. After she got married, she and her husband worked there in mission for many years. She helped train teachers and worked with women's groups in the church. After her husband died, she decided to get more training herself and to teach school back in the United States.

Now that she has retired, she has stayed active in her church but doesn't like it when people draw special attention to what she does any more than she did when she was in mission overseas. People who are working in mission usually don't get paid a lot, so the amount of money that is put aside for their retirement sometimes isn't enough for them to live on very comfortably. But because the church wants to thank them for the work they have done, people can support those who have worked in mission through giving to the Christmas Joy Offering. Half of the money we give will go to the Board of Pensions to help people who have worked for the church and find they don't have quite enough

money to get by. The other half goes to the racial ethnic schools supported by the Presbyterian Church (U.S.A.).

Ann Crane was a missionary in the Congo during the 1960s.

SCRIPTURE

So if anyone is in Christ, there is a new creation: everything old has passed away; see, everything has become new! (2 Corinthians 5:17).

MISSION AROUND THE WORLD

Sierra Leone

Sierra Leone is on the western coast of Africa between Guinea and Liberia. Find it on the map on page 110. The country had a ten-year civil war. Now there is peace, but the country needs healing. The Council of Churches in Sierra Leone (CCSL) helped in paving the way for peace. Presbyterian Disaster Assistance and the Presbyterian Hunger Program of the PC(USA) are funding a program that the CCSL runs. The program serves those most seriously affected by the war—women and children. Projects of this program are designed to fit the interests of people in each community. If they are interested in farming, CCSL might help them find seeds and tools, or find a blacksmith to make tools, or supply goats to the community. The CCSL program helps with the renewal of the country and with the renewal of the hearts, souls, and minds of those recovering from the war and its effects.

Giving What You Have

Give 5 cents for every Christmas gift you received to the church on Sunday.

What You Can Do

Consider all the things you have done to help missions this year. Look at your mission tree to see how many leaves have "grown" this year. And get ready for your new *2005 Children's Mission Yearbook!*

Craft

Cote d' Ivoire Bird Mask

In many parts of Central and West Africa, as well as among the Yupik people of Arctic Alaska, the mask is an important part of celebrations. The Yupik people say their masks are "our way of making prayer." You can make a mask from a paper plate, markers, paints, and any interesting objects that you have—feathers, very small shells, yarn, cord, stones, twigs, and leaves.

If you want, you can cut the paper plate into a shape you like. Be sure to cut a slit or holes for your eyes if you are going to wear the mask. Decorate your mask, then wear it or hang it up on the wall.

MISSION IN THE UNITED STATES

Presbytery of Yukon

Alaska

Look for the Presbytery of Yukon on the map on page 112. In that huge space, twenty-two churches spread out among majestic mountains and rivers. Nine of the churches are located in remote areas. In Alaska, remote means that the only way to get there is by airplane, snowmobile, boat, or even dogsled. The nine churches are not connected by any road system. The members of these churches worship God in four different languages: English, Korean, Inupiaq Eskimo, and Siberian Yupik Eskimo.

Across the Bering Strait, you'll see Russia on the map. Native lay pastors and mission workers from the Yukon take the gospel to Russia and minister in villages. Natives on St. Lawrence Island and across the waters in Russia speak the same Siberian Yupik language, making it easier to share God's word and God's love. People on both sides want to preserve their culture and native language. Prayers from many people support the mission. Prayer groups in the little village churches as well as the larger urban churches see prayer as the way to fulfill God's call.

The Jubilee Singers are members of Kuukpik Presbyterian Church in Nuiqsut, Alaska, one of the nine churches in remote areas.

PRAYER

God, we thank you for all that you do in missions here in the United States and around the world. Renew our spirits this New Year and give us new eyes to see and new ears to hear the needs of others. In Jesus' name. Amen.

Did You Know?

Some Yupik songs are about hunting because the Yupik people are traditional hunters and gatherers. They hunt walrus and sea mammals, fish for salmon, and gather eggs and berries. Yupik dances tell stories, sometimes about hunting and even about ice fishing. Yupik dancers wear costumes called *kuspuks* that look like winter coats. They use dance fans and sometimes wear masks.

Word of the Week Renewal

Renewal means to start over or to make something like new. The good news of God's love gives many people a new start.

Did You Know?

In a few days, we'll begin a NEW year. Let's reNEW our prayers and promises for mission in the United States and all around the world.

Presbyterian Church (U.S.A.) Partners Around the World

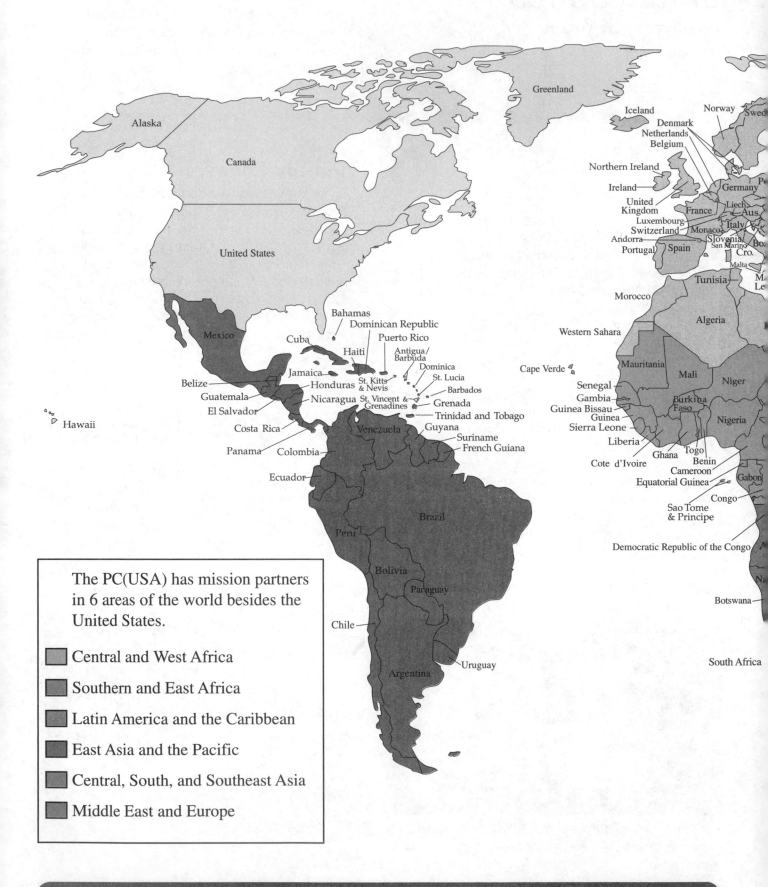

Greenland

Iceland
Norway
Swed
Denmark
Netherlands
Belgium

Alaska

Canada

Northern Ireland
Ireland
Germany
United Kingdom
France
Luxembourg
Switzerland
Andorra
Portugal
Spain
San Marino
Liech
Aus.
Italy
Monaco
Slovenia
Bo
Cro.
Malta
M.
Le

United States

Tunisia

Morocco

Mexico

Bahamas
Dominican Republic
Cuba
Puerto Rico
Haiti
Antigua/Barbuda
Dominica
Jamaica
St. Lucia

Belize
Honduras
St. Kitts & Nevis
Barbados
Guatemala
Nicaragua
St. Vincent & Grenadines
Grenada
El Salvador
Trinidad and Tobago

Costa Rica
Guyana
Suriname
French Guiana

Hawaii

Panama
Colombia
Venezuela

Ecuador

Western Sahara
Algeria

Cape Verde
Mauritania
Mali
Niger
Senegal
Gambia
Burkina Faso
Guinea Bissau
Guinea
Nigeria
Sierra Leone
Liberia
Cote d'Ivoire
Ghana
Togo
Benin
Cameroon
Equatorial Guinea
Gabon
Congo
Sao Tome & Principe

Democratic Republic of the Congo

Brazil

Peru

Bolivia

Paraguay

Botswana

Chile

Uruguay

Argentina

South Africa

The PC(USA) has mission partners in 6 areas of the world besides the United States.

- [ ] Central and West Africa
- [ ] Southern and East Africa
- [ ] Latin America and the Caribbean
- [ ] East Asia and the Pacific
- [ ] Central, South, and Southeast Asia
- [ ] Middle East and Europe

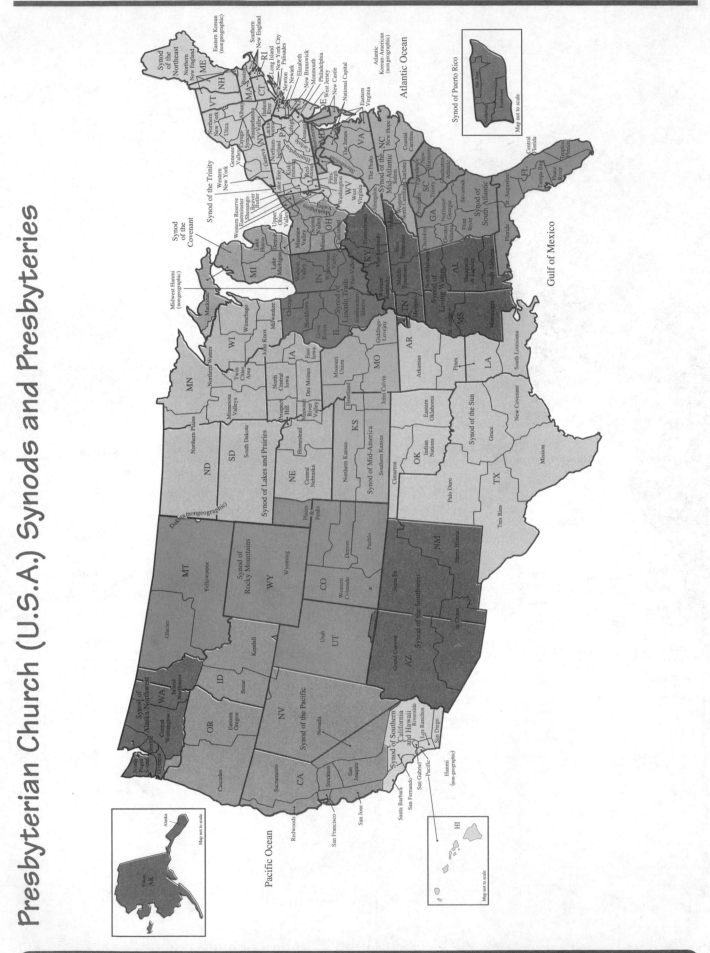